CRITICAL STUDIES OF
KEY TEXTS

James Joyce's
A Portrait of the Artist as a Young Man

Other titles available in the series

Liz Bellamy
Jonathan Swift's Gulliver's Travels

Nicola Bradbury
Charles Dickens' Great Expectations

David Fuller
James Joyce's Ulysses

Pauline Nestor
Charlotte Bronte's Jane Eyre

Suzanne Raitt
Virginia Woolf's To the Lighthouse

Gene Ruoff
Jane Austen's Sense and Sensibility

David Seed
James Joyce's A Portrait of the Artist as a Young Man

T. R. Wright
George Eliot's Middlemarch

CRITICAL STUDIES OF
KEY TEXTS

James Joyce's
A Portrait of the Artist as a Young Man

David Seed
Liverpool University

St. Martin's Press
New York

All rights reserved. For information, write:
Scholarly and Reference Division,
St. Martin's Press, Inc.,
175 Fifth Avenue, New York, NY 10010

First published in the United States of America in 1992

Printed in Great Britain

ISBN 0–312–08426–9 (cloth)
ISBN 0–312–08600–8 (pbk)

Library of Congress Cataloging-in-Publication Data

Seed, David.
    James Joyce's A portrait of the artist as a young
        man / David Seed
    p.   cm. — (Critical studies of key texts)
    Includes bibliographical references and index.
    ISBN 0–312–08426–9 (cloth).
    ISBN 0–312–08600–8 (pbk).
    1. Joyce, James, 1882–1941. Portrait of the artist as
a young man.   I. Title.   II. Series.
PR6019.09P6484 1992   92–14962
823'912—dc20   CIP

Contents

Acknowledgements

I am grateful to Liverpool University for a research grant and for a period of study leave to complete this book; and also to my friend and colleague Bernard Beatty for helpful discussions on Catholic ritual and belief. Acknowledgement is made to Jonathan Cape for British Commonwealth and world permission from James Joyce's *Stephen Hero* and *A Portrait of the Artist as a Young Man*. I also acknowledge US permission from Viking Penguin, a division of Penguin Books USA, to publish extracts from *A Portrait of the Artist* (copyright 1916 by B. W. Huebsch, 1944 by Nora Barnacle, and 1964 by the Estate of James Joyce) and from the Society of Authors to publish extracts from *Stephen Hero*. Lastly, I should like to thank Barbara Smith for typing the manuscript.

Preface

Joyce's title *A Portrait of the Artist as a Young Man* announces the application of an analogy from one artistic medium to another. The topos of the novel as portrait had become well established by the 1880s. Robert Louis Stevenson's essay 'A note on realism' (1883) bases itself on a sustained comparison between picture and story, and Henry James responded to Stevenson's stress on execution in his collection of critical essays *Partial Portraits* (1888). Here, especially in 'The art of fiction', James applied the portrait analogy polemically to counter a perceived puritanism in British culture. Because the public had become so used to encountering art within galleries James attempted to move outside the frame and suggest common criteria of form.[1] More importantly, since it was to suggest Joyce's own title, *The Portrait of a Lady* (1880–1) explores a notion of the self rather more complex than that suggested in the title. Madame Merle, specifically identified as the most intelligent character in the novel, makes the following declaration to the protagonist, which is later substantiated by the methods of the novel: 'There's no such thing as an isolated man or woman; we're each of us made up of some cluster of appurtenances. What shall we call our "self"? ... It overflows into everything that belongs to us – and then it flows back again.'[2] These assertions destabilise the self, articulating it as a dynamic principle far less fixed than the body or the self's possessions.

When he came to write his 1904 essay which was the first sketch for his novel Joyce followed a similar line of argument. Although he retains the term 'portrait' in his title his opening statement tacitly questions its adequacy: 'the features of infancy are not commonly reproduced in the adolescent portrait.'[3] As in James's novel an argument is mounted against the suggestions of fixity and stasis in the portrait analogy. The young Joyce, of course, writes more adversarially against conventionalised notions of depiction and he does this, like Madame Merle, by undermining assumptions of stability. The essay posits notions of flux ('rhythm', 'curve', 'fluid succession of presents') against static terms ('iron memorial', 'beards') which carry misleading suggestions of solidity. Joyce's new emphasis obviously relates to changes in painting as much as to changes in novel theory. Indeed, the one was clearly feeding off the other. Oscar Wilde, for instance, praised Pater's *Imaginary Portraits* (1887) for being the work of an 'intellectual impressionist', and then went on to apply this awareness in *The Picture of Dorian Gray* (1891) which was to have a direct influence on the middle sections of Joyce's novel.[4] The former examines the social and moral dimensions to seeing and being seen by reversing the conventional relation of portrait to subject.[5] Wilde's title refers both to the focal object within the narrative and to the novel's own processes of depiction.

Joyce, on the other hand, repeatedly associates portraits with authority and uses them to punctuate the phases of Stephen's shifting relation to his culture. In Chapter 1 he walks along the corridor at Clongowes towards the rector's office, passing the portraits of Jesuit worthies which encourage Stephen's temporary sense of participating in history. By Chapter 2, however, the stability associated with such objects comes into question as his family moves from house to house. Symptomatically, the portraits are taken down from the walls. Chapter 3 replaces them with an idealised image of the Virgin Mary which is vocalised in so far as it seems to address Stephen's imagination. And in the final chapter sacred and profane icons are contrasted, a print of the Sacred Heart and a photograph of the czar. The latter occasions a heated argument between Stephen and another student over the limits of secular authority. In other words the 'portrait' of the title becomes pluralised and written into the narrative as possessing voices, thereby rendering the solicitations of Stephen's surrounding culture.

It is a truism that this interaction between self and context can only be expressed in words and yet *A Portrait* again and again articulates Stephen's growth as a clash between voices. Despite the novel's title, it is very difficult to visualise Stephen; we have a much stronger sense of him as a speaker. In 1920 Joyce disclaimed any interest in painting (except, significantly, portraiture); on the other hand, his interest in drama is a matter of documented fact (E, 491). It is hardly surprising that the admirer of Ibsen, D'Annunzio, Synge and other dramatists should render Stephen's growing consciousness as an engagement with the voices of his culture. This is where the theories of Mikhail Bakhtin offer profitable avenues for examining *A Portrait*. Bakhtin's starting point lies in the proposition that 'discourse is a social phenomenon' (DI, 259). Because the individual is born into an already existing set of linguistic circumstances s/he must develop an identity through a capacity to take control of these available discourses. Utterance, therefore, becomes an 'active participant in such diversity' (DI, 272). It is astonishing that Bakhtin never refers to Joyce because, as David Lodge has pointed out, any reader 'will constantly be struck by the relevance of Bakhtin's criticism to the Irishman's writing'.[6] The notion of dialogics in particular helps us to understand Stephen Dedalus' struggle to appropriate a voice of his own. This struggle involves him in manoeuvring through the political, religious and moral claims made on him, and Bakhtin's theories help us to recognise that even the most intimate areas of Stephen's thoughts are made up of the expressions and vocabulary of those around him. Even in its heyday the pictorial analogy was never, *could* never, be straightforwardly visual when applied to the novel. Bakhtin helps us to articulate the sheer extent to which Joyce exploits voice, utterance, speech register and language in *A Portrait* to dramatise the different stages of Stephen's growth.

Abbreviations

CH Robert H. Denning, *James Joyce: The critical heritage. Volume One: 1902–1927*, London: Routledge & Kegan Paul, 1970.

CW James Joyce, *The Critical Writings*, ed. by Ellsworth Mason and Richard Ellmann, London: Faber, 1959.

DI Mikhail Bakhtin, *The Dialogic Imagination: Four essays*, trans. by Michael Holquist and Caryl Emerson, Austin TX: University of Texas Press, 1981.

E Richard Ellmann, *James Joyce*, rev. edn, Oxford and New York: Oxford University Press, 1982.

G Don Gifford, *Notes for Joyce: 'Dubliners' and 'A Portrait of the Artist as a Young Man'*, New York: E. P. Dutton, 1967.

K Robert B. Kershner, *Joyce, Bakhtin, and Popular Literature*, Chapel Hill NC: University of North Carolina Press, 1989.

P James Joyce, *A Portrait of the Artist as a Young Man: The definitive text*, ed. by Richard Ellmann, London: Jonathan Cape, 1975.

SG Mikhail Bakhtin, *Speech Genres and Other Late Essays*, trans. by Vern W. McGee, ed. by Caryl Emerson and Michael Holquist, Austin TX: University of Texas Press, 1986.

SH James Joyce, *Stephen Hero*, ed. by Theodore Spencer, rev. edn, London: Jonathan Cape, 1969.

U James Joyce, *Ulysses: The corrected text*, ed. by Hans Walter Gabler, student edn, Harmondsworth: Penguin, 1986.

I

Contexts

Historical and Cultural Context

COMPOSITION AND PUBLICATION

Early in 1904 Joyce wrote a short autobiographical story entitled 'A portrait of the artist' (reprinted in the 1962 and 1973 Casebooks) but his efforts to get it published came to nothing. Nothing daunted, by the following year Joyce was well into a longer autobiographical novel to be called, at his brother's suggestion, *Stephen Hero*. The year 1908 saw him revising this text even though he was losing faith in the project. He then made a fresh start on what was to become *A Portrait of the Artist as a Young Man* and completed it in 1914. Joyce's retention of the dateline 'Dublin 1904 – Trieste 1914' at the end of the published novel makes it clear that he saw *A Portrait* as the culmination of a compositional process which had gone through three phases. *A Portrait of the Artist as a Young Man* was serialised in *The Egoist* from 7 February 1914 to 1 September 1915. Afraid of prosecution under the obscenity laws, the printers made a number of deletions in the later episodes which Joyce insisted should be restored in the book. In common with his other fiction Joyce had great difficulty in getting the novel published. It was rejected by many publishers including Cape, whose reader Edward Garnett described the book as 'formless'. The novel was finally published in the United States by B. W. Huebsch on 29 December 1916; and in Britain from the American sheets by the Egoist Press on 2 February 1917. In 1964 Chester G. Anderson (with Richard Ellmann's assistance) compared the Dublin manuscript of *A Portrait* with existing editions and with all the corrections made as planned by Joyce. The result was the Viking Compass Edition, which has since been the definitive text of the novel.

CONTEXT

In the early 1900s while he was teaching English in Trieste, Joyce would express the following sentiments about his native country: 'The government sowed hunger, syphilis, superstition, and alcoholism there; puritans, Jesuits, and bigots have sprung up.' Negative as this sounds, it tells only half the story, for Joyce continued: 'in spite of everything Ireland remains the brain of the United Kingdom' (E, 217). Joyce's indignation over Irish subservience to two rulers – the Pope and the British monarch – grew out of a tendency to identify his destiny with that of Ireland. Far from being indifferent to the country of his birth, Joyce was closely involved in the cultural ferment of the 1890s and carefully followed the events leading up to Irish independence. Not surprisingly, his works bear countless signs of their cultural context.

The Irish Literary Theatre was formed, as Joyce admitted, to protest against the 'sterility and falsehood of the modern stage' and on 8 June 1899 there took place one of the key events in its history – the premiere of W. B. Yeats's *The Countess Cathleen* (CW, 69–70). A group of students booed and hissed the production, with the conspicuous exception of Joyce, who clapped loudly. The reviewers' hostility to the play evidently matched that of most students. The *Daily Nation* complained at its 'hideous caricature of our people's mental and moral character' and Francis Skeffington

(McCann in *A Portrait*) wrote a letter 'to protest an art . . . which offers as a type of our people a loathsome brood of apostates' (G, 175). Joyce refused to sign this letter just as Stephen refuses to sign the petition to the czar in *A Portrait*. Joyce's active resistance to this public hostility is transformed into a passive disengagement in the novel. Speculating on the symbolism of birds, some lines from the Countess's death speech in Yeats's play come to mind and they in turn remind him of the première night: 'He was alone at the side of the balcony, looking out of jaded eyes at the culture of Dublin in the stalls and at the tawdry scenecloths and human dolls framed by the garish lamps of the stage' (*P*, 231). An implicit contrast emerges between the jeers of the other students and Stephen's silence, but more importantly the separation of observer from observed looks forward to Stephen's final departure from Dublin and renders in miniature his withdrawal from Irish culture.

The promotion of the Abbey Theatre formed part of a wider cause championed by Yeats: the creation of an Irish literature in English which would take its rightful part among the cultures of Europe and which would inspire national pride in its people. To this end he had founded the Irish Literary Society of London in 1891 and the National Literary Society the following year. However, he failed to recognise the deep conservatism of the nationalist cause which revealed itself in the disturbances over *The Countess Cathleen* and Synge's two plays *In the Shadow of the Glen* (1903) and *The Playboy of the Western World* (1907). The emerging attitude has been summed up by the historian F. S. L. Lyons: 'A theatre, or a play, or a book, or a poem that claimed to be "national" would be judged according to whether or not it conformed to the stereotype which ascribed to Catholic Ireland the virtues of purity, innocence, and sanctity'.[1] This attitude gives a revisionist irony to Stephen's reflection in *A Portrait* that the peasant woman Davin meets is a 'type of her race . . . calling the stranger to her bed' (*P*, 186–7); and it is converted into comic theatre in the Circe episode of *Ulysses* when Bloom undergoes a mock trial for corrupting Irish womanhood. Stern moral disapproval, still with nationalistic implications, was expressed by at least two Irish reviewers of *A Portrait*. While both acknowledged Joyce's skill, the *Freeman's Journal* complained that 'Mr. Joyce plunges and drags the reader after him into the slime of foul sewers', and the *Irish Book Lover* leapt to paternal protection by protesting that 'no clean-minded person could possibly allow it to remain within reach of his wife, his sons or daughters' (*CH*.I, 98, 102). This presumption of purity with its attendant limitation of literature to the ideal or celebratory gave Joyce an implicit target, which he attacked relentlessly in *Dubliners*, *A Portrait* and *Ulysses*.

Coincidentally, the 1890s were a key decade both for the Irish literary revival and for Joyce's own literary development, although the two moved in opposite directions. Douglas Hyde, the president of the Gaelic League and of the Irish Texts Society (which began publishing its volumes in 1899) argued in the preface to his *Literary History of Ireland* that ancient Irish literature was still influencing contemporary Ireland through its store of folk traditions. Joyce was profoundly suspicious of any such collective entity and objected to Yeats's plays for their use of folklore. At a time when emphasis was being put on native literature Joyce made a point of developing his reading in an opposite cosmopolitan direction. At University College (a hot-bed of Gaelic League activity in the late 1890s) he studied French and Italian, and his omnivorous reading included the works of Hauptmann, Verlaine, Tolstoy and D'Annunzio. Not only was this reading taking Joyce into continental culture but his discovery of Ibsen acted as a catalyst for the formation of one of his most cherished beliefs: the necessary opposition between the artist and society.

The signs of this belief emerge in Joyce's writings as early as 1899, when he praised Michael Munkacsy's painting *Ecce Homo* for its dramatic force. Christ has been humanised and thereby set in opposition to the crowd confronting him. Indeed, it is this opposition which fascinates Joyce. On the one hand it involves the 'drama of the thrice told revolt of humanity against a great teacher'; on the other it involves Christ's aloof defiance of the crowd (*CW*, 36). The following year Joyce delivered a paper entitled 'Drama and life' to the college's Literary and Historical Society. This brought him into conflict with the college censors but also gave him an opportunity to formulate an artistic position using Ibsen as a springboard. Once again opposition emerges as the keynote but this time the vocabulary of conflict becomes more strident. Because it is uniquely privileged as a literary mode concerned with truth and freedom (significantly, not necessarily with beauty), 'drama will be for the future at war with convention, if it is to realize itself truly'. The better the drama the more the artist's role approaches the sacerdotal: 'the artist forgoes his very self and stands a mediator in awful truth before the veiled face of God' (*CW*, 41, 42). Joyce had read Shaw's *Quintessence of Ibsenism* (1891) and must have been well aware that he was championing a controversial figure. He even tried to interest the Irish Literary Theatre in producing *When We Dead Awaken* and *Hedda Gabler*, but without success.

A polemical vigour informs several of Joyce's essays and reviews from the early 1900s, which are fuelled by a determination not to bow to unacceptable orthodoxies. Although he had frequented socialist meetings in Dublin, when reviewing the poems of William Rooney, one of the founders of Sinn Fein, Joyce attacked his attempts to substitute patriotism for skill and declared roundly that the poetry of the national movement was 'work which has an interest of the day, but collectively it has not a third part of the value of the work of a man like Mangan' (*CW*, 91). This review infuriated Arthur Griffith, the editor of the nationalist *United Irishman* and main founder of the movement. The fact that Joyce came to have stronger and stronger reservations about Mangan is scarcely relevant here to the contrast Joyce establishes between the individual and the collective. This tension is explored in 'The day of the rabblement', a piece Joyce wrote for a new college magazine. When it and an essay by Skeffington advocating women's rights in the university were rejected by the clerical authorities both were printed privately as a pamphlet. In his essay Joyce attacks the Irish as the 'most belated race in Europe' and proclaims: 'A nation which never advanced so far as a miracle-play affords no literary model to the artist, and he must look abroad' (*CW*, 70). This piece takes artistic isolation as its premise and simultaneously predicts both Joyce's own exile and the internal dialectics of *A Portrait*. Arthur Clery, who had earlier attacked his paper on Ibsen, similarly denounced Joyce in coy mock-Elizabethan terms as being 'corrupted ... by the learning of Italie or othere foreigne parts'; and several years later denounced divided allegiances: 'No man can have two countries .... What a man looks upon as his country usually appears from the language he uses' (i.e. from the way he uses terms like 'nation' and 'history') (E, 90).[2] Given the increasing hostility of Joyce's critical writings, it is no surprise that he should have tried his hand at satire. 'The Holy Office' (1904) is a broadside ballad attacking what he saw as the 'anemic spirituality' of writers like Yeats and Russell. Borrowing Aristotle's term for tragic effect Joyce casts himself as 'Katharsis – Purgative', verbalising a function which drains off the physicality the Irish aesthetes refuse to recognise: 'Thus I relieve their timid arses, / Perform my office of Katharsis' (*CW*, 151). The ballad skips nimbly between the sacred and the profane, linking spirituality with sexual prudery and tacitly promoting the cause of frank physical expression in literature. Here again we anticipate *A Portrait*'s ironies against Stephen's aesthetic intensities.

It would be a mistake to conclude that Joyce simply rejected all contemporary Irish writing. He retained a respect for Yeats, whom he regarded as the greatest living Irish poet, a respect demonstrated by allusions to his works in *A Portrait* and *Ulysses*, offset by a scepticism towards the notion of a pool of folk culture. During their meeting in 1902, when Joyce questioned Yeats about his interest in folklore, the older poet replied that he found the collective rural imagination a welcome antidote to the urban isolation of the artist. For all their differences Yeats played a crucial role in Joyce's career. Although he rejected *Exiles*, he invited Joyce to write a new work for the Irish theatre, which the latter agreed to, but without result. Much more importantly, Yeats introduced Joyce's work to Ezra Pound and thereby gave him an entry into Modernist circles. Now Joyce had at least a small and appreciative readership from fellow artists like Wyndham Lewis and Ford Maddox Hueffer, both of whom responded warmly to *A Portrait*. The other Irish writer who influenced him most strongly at this time seems to have been George Moore, whom Ernest Boyd (in his *Ireland's Literary Renaissance*, 1916) identified as Joyce's precursor and an important cosmopolitan presence on the Irish literary scene. Moore introduced Joyce to Dujardin's use of the interior monologue which, Joyce later admitted, had a profound impact on the composition of *Ulysses*. The career which Moore outlined in his autobiography, *Confessions of a Young Man* (1888), bears a close similarity to Joyce's own. Both writers had an early enthusiasm for Shelley, championed Ibsen, confronted the censorship laws and went into exile in Paris. Above all, *Confessions* establishes itself dialogically as a prolonged attack on conventions, a 'moral revolt against any action that could or would definitely compromise' his passion for art. Moore looks forward to Stephen Dedalus in his formulation of an adversarial artistic stance, a posture of sustained conflict with 'conventionalities': 'The life of the artist should be a practical protest against the so-called decencies of life.'[3] One means which Moore uses of articulating protest is through his insistent repetition of the pronoun 'I', thereby giving priority to the individual at the expense of social or moral claims. Joyce, as we shall see, even in *Stephen Hero* sets the declarations of his protagonist in a rhetorical context which at once endorses the latter's attacks on convention and ironically examines those attacks.

Moore undoubtedly accelerated Joyce's decision to leave Ireland, which was taken for a combination of reasons. He was in a sense imitating the pattern of respected literary predecessors like Dante and Ibsen; but he was also following a national tradition of emigration referred to in the song Stephen's father sings in Cork. Joyce was exchanging one metropolis for another with its community of exiled artists in Paris and he would constantly be drawn to cities like Zurich and Trieste which had culturally mixed populations. *A Portrait* refers variously to French, Italian, German, Latin and Norwegian, but it was not until 1932 that Joyce could translate the same poem (significantly an Irish one – James Stephen's 'Stephen's Green') into all these languages. Such polyglot ease lies in the possible future of *A Portrait* beyond the limits of its narrative. It is part of the promise of exile, but such an aim met with grim disapproval by the nationalists at home. Arthur Griffith declared roundly in the *United Irishman* for 17 October 1903: 'Cosmopolitanism never produced a great artist nor a good man yet and never will.'[4] Joyce for his part, whose whole career was directed towards giving the lie to the first part of Griffith's claim, baulked at the nationalists' championing of Gaelic, although he respected their attempts to give Ireland economic independence. In November 1906 he confessed to his brother: 'If the Irish programme did not insist on the Irish language I suppose I could call myself a nationalist. As it is, I am content to recognize an exile: and, prophetically, a repudiated one.'[5]

The events of *A Portrait* span roughly a decade from the death of Parnell in 1891 (which Yeats saw in his *Autobiographies* as the starting date for modern Irish literature) to the rise of nationalist fervour around the turn of the century. Stephen's resistance to the pressures of clerical authority and public opinion have a clear continuity with the argument over Parnell's fate at the Christmas dinner. Here Stephen's father vociferously laments the latter's betrayal by the clergy and the Irish people, and it is no exaggeration to say that Parnell's memory persists throughout *A Portrait*. In his study, *Joyce's Politics* (1980), Daniel Manganiello stresses the extent of Joyce's political reading and involvement in cultural debate, and he extrapolates the following analogy from *A Portrait*: 'Stephen perceives his role as that of a martyr for his art as Parnell was a martyr for the national cause.'[6] And Malcolm Brown puts the case even more strongly, arguing that Joyce 'froze history at the instant of the Parnellite disaster'.[7] Parnell, in other words, functions as a crypto-hero in *A Portrait*, the victim of a fickle and narrow-minded public, just as in his criticism Joyce records his indignation at the betrayals of Ibsen and Wilde by their respective societies. In his *Autobiographies* Yeats recalls the devotion offered at first to the 'solitary and proud Parnell' and notes that on the latter's demise the Irish press used the following quotation from Goethe: 'The Irish seem to me like a pack of hounds, always dragging down some noble stag.'[8] This analogy was adopted by Joyce, who claimed to have written a pamphlet on Parnell as early as 1891, and was used repeatedly in his early writings as an image of aristocratic disdain. In 1912 on the occasion of the passage through parliament of the third Home Rule bill Joyce wrote a tribute to this 'uncrowned king' for a Trieste newspaper called 'The shade of Parnell'. Here he ruminates with bemused relish on Parnell's apparent lack of qualifications for a nationalist leader – his Protestant aristocractic origins, his awkward rhetorical style and so on. It becomes clear that for Joyce Parnell was a heroic man of principle betrayed among other things by prudish hypocrisy over his liaison with Kitty O'Shea; and Joyce reserves his harshest sarcasm for the fact that Parnell was destroyed not by the English but by the very Irish for whom he was trying to achieve independence.

Once Joyce had taken up residence in Trieste his attitude towards Ireland appears to have mellowed with distance. In 1907 he gave three lectures on Irish topics, the last of which has been lost. The first of the series, 'Ireland, island of saints and sages', gives a reading of Irish history which would be quite congenial to nationalist interpretations of the country's literature. Indeed, Irish nationalism, he argues, represents the desire to 'renew under new forms the glory of a past civilization' and continues, with implicit self-justification, that 'no one who has any self-respect stays in Ireland, but flees afar as though from a country that has undergone the visitation of an angered Jove' (*CW*, 171). The earlier tug between the individual and her/his society has now become complicated to the extent that Joyce identifies himself with Irish culture ('*our* civilization is a vast fabric') and even presents himself as following a national tradition by going into exile. Now his quarrel is with Irish conditions as distinct from Irish culture, the former comprising the subject of his second lecture on Mangan; and, however indebted he might have been to Ezra Pound for getting *A Portrait* published, there is no reason to suppose that he would have endorsed Pound's harsh criticism of the Irish made in 1915, the year *A Portrait* was being serialised in *The Little Review*: 'I simply cannot accept the evidence that they have any worth *as a nation* or that they have any function in modern civilisation.'[9] Joyce would never go so far. His attack on the promotion of Gaelic in *Stephen Hero*, and in *Ulysses* his parody of Michael Cusack (the founder of the Gaelic Athletic Association) as the blustering Citizen, his burlesque of Robert Emmet's execution and his gibes against the nationalists' colour green are all consistent with a position argued in the Trieste lectures. Unlike Joyce's earliest reviews, the ironies are not simply directed against Ireland as such. Now he is attacking a narrow-minded (and in some cases racist) nationalism which does not recognise the layered nature of Irish history. It becomes a major concern of *Ulysses* to insist that Irish and particularly Dublin culture is cosmopolitan, a composite drawn from quite disparate sources. In *A Portrait* this has yet to come; the environment figures as a series of resistances to the protagonists' desires although the relation of the self to the discourses of its cultural context is a complex one.

Throughout his critical writing Joyce gives no sign of a native tradition of fiction which he could adapt to his own use. He was not interested in local colour or humoristic writing and commented scathingly on the sloppy attention to detail in George Moore's stories, *The Untilled Field* (1902). Instead, Joyce applied to Irish motifs methods culled from Flaubert, Dujardin and other continental authors. Joyce's contacts with the Modernists undoubtedly acted as a catalyst in shifting his fictional method away from the linear narrative of *Stephen Hero* to the complex progressions of *A Portrait*. Dorothy Van Ghent has argued that the emphasis on youth in turn-of-the-century fiction suggests a breakdown of cultural stability and sees autobiographical novels like *A Portrait* as raising questions such as the nature of art.[10] Joyce's novel for her traces out a breakdown in received cultural authority as embodied in Stephen's fathers, ecclesiastical and biological, and then enacts the protagonist's attempts to restructure meaning in his experience. In contrast with *Stephen Hero*, *A Portrait* sets up a multitude of voices which interact dialogically with each other. Discourse is thus pluralised and the various details of Stephen's environment (the recurring birds, colour contrasts between red and green, etc.) become charged with metaphorical significances relative to the phase of his experience where they occur. The startling discontinuities in the narrative can also be partly explained by their associative connections within Stephen's consciousness, which is accordingly privileged over predictable formal pattern. In that respect *A Portrait* can be usefully related to Modernist experiments in limited point of view by such writers as James, Conrad and Ford. And it is no coincidence that the phrase 'stream of consciousness' should first be applied to literature in 1918 in

13

the very journal which serialised *A Portrait*. Reviewing Dorothy Richardson's novels the philosopher–novelist May Sinclair described this new mode in negatives: 'there is no drama, no situation, no set scene. Nothing happens. It is just life going on and on. It is Miriam's stream of consciousness going on and on'.[11] This stark contrast between form and consciousness cannot stand as a plausible account, either of Richardson's work or of Joyce's novel, because it is impossible to conceive of expression not conferring structure, but its priorities do help to explain how what Hugh Kenner was to call 'theme-words' or 'controlling images' arise from the protagonist's own mental processes. *A Portrait* then applies the Modernistic methods Joyce learned in the early 1900s to a subject growing out of the ferment of Irish cultural politics in the 1890s.

Critical Reception of the Text

An adequate survey of the criticism of *A Portrait* would need a monograph in itself and the following has been necessarily selective. I have concentrated on those critical writings which carry implications for the novel as a whole rather than specific motifs or scenes. For an excellent overview of the criticism up to the mid-1970s, the reader is referred to Thomas F. Staley and Bernard Benstock's 'Strings in the Labyrinth', the first chapter to their 1976 anthology *Approaches to Joyce's 'Portrait'*. For a thorough listing of criticism up to 1977 the reader cannot do better than consult the second edition of Robert H. Deming's *Bibliography of James Joyce Studies*. Full details of the works cited in this section can be found either in the Notes or in the Bibliography

The reviewers' reactions to *A Portrait* on its publication in 1916 were divided between recognition of its obvious artistic skill and defensive recoils from its subject-matter. H. G. Wells struck the characteristic note in the *Nation* when he praised the book's sensory immediacy and experimental structure but diagnosed a 'cloacal obsession' (*CH*.I, 86). The *Manchester Guardian* expressed distinct unease about Stephen's 'passion for foul-smelling things', whereas *Everyman* threw moderation to the winds by declaring: 'Mr. Joyce is a clever wordist, but we feel he would be really at his best in a treatise on drains!' (*CH*.I, 93, 85). While the reviewers seemed unsure whether to classify this kind of writing as realistic or impressionistic the source of their hostility can be traced to Joyce's deliberate thwarting of expectations of decorum or moral uplift. The *Freeman's Journal* was unusually explicit in identifying this anti-idealistic tendency in the novel, complaining that Joyce's 'pen, instead of pointing to the stars overhead, is degraded into a muck-rake' (*CH*.I, 98). Not surprisingly, since he had played a major role in having a *A Portrait* serialised in *The Egoist*, Ezra Pound's review for that same journal was refreshingly free from expressions of genteel distaste. He singled out for special praise the novel's disciplined clarity and initiated a whole tradition in Joyce criticism by pointing out a debt to a French forebear when he claimed that the novel was the 'nearest thing to Flaubertian prose that we have now in English' (*CH*.I, 83).

Although Joyce figures in such studies as Joseph Warren Beach's *The Twentieth Century Novel* (1932) the beginning of Joyce criticism is usually dated at 1930 with Stuart Gilbert's monograph *James Joyce's 'Ulysses'* and at 1944 with the appearance of Harry Levin's critical analysis, *James Joyce*. Whereas Levin locates a portrait within the European tradition of the *Künstlerroman*, Breon Mitchell (1976) has categorised it as a *Bildungsroman* (a 'novel of development') which makes a critique of the genre.[1] Levin's other rather more important point about *The Portrait* is that rhythm, imagery, etc. constitute a 'presentational continuum' geared to Stephen's growth. This simple but crucial proposition was more or less echoed by Marvin Magalaner in his pioneering study of Joyce's early fiction, *Time of Apprenticeship* (1959), where he argues that the impressionistic style traces out the rhythm of Stephen's perceptions. Richard Ellmann's biography, *James Joyce* (1959, revised 1982), further elaborates the notion of growth by applying Joyce's own analogy with a development from the embryo stage (E, 297–8). Images, scenes and even individual words pass through a process of incremental elaboration or, as Ellmann summarises the novel, 'the book moves from rudimentary meanings to more complex ones.' Although Ellmann does not have the space to develop this point, it nevertheless marks an important step forward in accounting for the curious mobility of the text of *A Portrait*.

It was this mobility which received outstanding analysis in *Dublin's Joyce* (1955), where Hugh Kenner draws an extended analogy with the counterpointing of melody against harmony. Starting from the apparent overstatement that 'the entire lifework of James Joyce is stated on the first two pages of the *Portrait*', he proceeds to demonstrate an intricate but totally convincing series of word-associations. Sections are given their coherence by controlling images which both revise and exceed preceding ones. For Kenner the special achievement of the novel lies in the fact that 'Joyce can cause patterns of words to make up the very moral texture of Stephen's mind.' In his essay Kenner raises a whole range of issues which have been taken up by later critics: Joyce's perspective on Stephen; the novel's use of symbolism and leitmotifs; and, not least, the question of the book's structure. The latter, he tells us, is based on the pattern of 'dream nourished in contempt of reality, put into practice, and dashed by reality'. Kenner also differentiates between the odd-numbered chapters, whose theme is 'ego vs authority', and the others, which deal with 'Dublin as the dream'.[2] In 1976, considering the relation of *A Portrait* to Cubism, Kenner added one major revision to his original essay: namely, that the novel's perspective was mobile not fixed. By this new account Stephen emerges not from description so much as from an 'interaction between the changing subject' and the 'changing viewpoint'.[3] The reader, in other words, is compelled to revise her/his sense of Stephen as the novel progresses.

One of the many valuable insights Kenner offers is a warning against applying the notion of stream of consciousness to *A Portrait* because it is too reductive to cope with the variety of styles. Ironically, Melvin Friedman (*Stream of*

Consciousness, 1955) admits as much in his self-contradictory attempt to relate the novel to the stream-of-consciousness tradition. Both Friedman and many other Joyce critics have struggled to articulate the continuity of *A Portrait* and from the late 1950s through the 1960s numerous essays appeared on roses, eyes, hands and in short any conceivable example of what used to be called 'lines of imagery'. One of the best readings in this area is Bernard Benstock's 'A light from some other world' (in *Approaches*), which avoids the pitfall of narrowness by considering various examples of verbal repetition and variation. Benstock's symbolistic commentary has useful local insights to offer (on, for instance, the sexual dimension to eye-contact) and he demonstrates a strategic confusion of the sacred with the profane, the connections between bird symbolism and the Daedalus myth, and so on. In a different area Grant H. Redford's 1958 essay 'The role of structure in Joyce's *Portrait*' (collected in Morris and Nault's 1962 *Casebook*) hypothesises a search throughout Joyce's career for a perfect order achieved through the interweaving of symbols and motifs. *A Portrait* enacts the search which concludes with an appropriately long final section because here Stephen has liberated himself and proportionately gained in self-confidence.

Redford sets his face against Hugh Kenner's insistence that Joyce establishes an ironic perspective on Stephen, but it was not until the publication of Wayne C. Booth's *The Rhetoric of Fiction* (1961) that perspective became identified as a problem. Drawing comparisons with Defoe and Swift, Booth puts *A Portrait* forward as a case of what can happen when narrative irony is inadequately signalled and when our prolonged intimacy with a character smothers our capacity for judgement. Joyce's novel, he argues, suffers from its own objective method by being absolutely ambiguous in the perspective levelled on Stephen. With the villanelle episode Booth complains: 'are we to smile at Stephen or pity him in his tortured longings?' In effect, he conflates a number of issues here: first, there is the oddly Victorian assumption that the reader's task is to pass judgement on the protagonist; then Booth arbitrarily rules out the possibility of a mixed tone as perspective; and finally he rules narrative implication out of court as a direct result of his preference for a rhetoric which dots its i's: 'wherever explicit judgement has been unavailable, critical troubles, as well as some extraordinary delights, have ensued.'[4] Partly because the general concept of point of view has been given so much prominence in Anglo-American criticism many writers on *A Portrait* have lined themselves up in the opposing camps of the ironists as against the non-ironists. S. L. Goldberg, for instance, explicitly endorses Kenner and sees welcoming signs at the end of the novel that Stephen is 'beginning to turn his critical intelligence upon himself', that is, that he is now participating in the overall ironic awareness of the novel itself.[5] The debate over perspective has bedevilled criticism of *A Portrait* and reduced it to a 'pro and con' rhetoric ultimately as arid as the argument over the existence of the ghosts in *The Turn of the Screw*. Apart from anything else, this concentration distracted attention from critically productive areas like a consideration of the novel's social context. It was not until 1980 that Gérard Genette in his *Narrative Discourse* suggested a way out of this impasse by distinguishing between the questions 'Who sees?' and 'Who speaks?', thereby shifting the focus of debate on to discourse.[6]

The 1960s was partly a decade of consolidation in Joyce criticism and in that period a number of anthologies of essays on *A Portrait* were published, unfortunately with considerable duplication. One of the best in terms of compiling a diversity of primary and secondary materials was William E. Morris and Clifford A. Nault's *Casebook* (1962), which includes pieces from Joyce's own early writings as well as over twenty essays grouped according to topics. Arnold Goldman's *The Joyce Paradox* (1966) participates in the same general impulse behind these collections by attempting to synthesise the diverse approaches to Joyce. Side-stepping the issues of perspective, he wags his finger over some of the facile identifications in symbolist readings, and argues instead that Joyce invites mutually opposing interpretations by positioning Stephen on a knife-edge between success and failure. C. H. Peake's *James Joyce: The citizen and the artist* (1977) and Matthew Hodgart's *James Joyce: A student's guide* (1978) do not even attempt a synthesis of criticism in their attempts to appeal to a non-specialist reader. In practice this means that Peake repeats many by now familiar points about recurrent motifs, Stephen's emergence, etc.; and Hodgart tilts his anyway brief discussion of *A Portrait* towards moralism by commenting on the cost of Stephen's severing ties with family and country, and towards formal confusion by referring to the novel as an 'autobiography'.

Two specific areas of *A Portrait* have received extended critical discussion which bears on the organisation of the novel as a whole: Joyce's notion of epiphanies and Stephen Dedalus' statements on aesthetics. The former has been greatly accelerated since the publication of *Stephen Hero* in 1944 and O. A. Silverman's edition of the *Epiphanies* in 1956. Irene Hendry Chayes' 1946 essay 'Joyce's Epiphanies' broke new ground and drew valuable distinctions between three kinds of ephiphany: 'the moment of revelation without its narrative base', the epiphany where we are first aware of its effect on the beholder, and a 'process of compression and distillation'.[7] Virtually every critic who writes on epiphany notes its centrality for Joyce's whole œuvre and for that matter its centrality to modern literature. This was the historical thesis of Morris Beja's *Epiphany in the Modern Novel* (1971), where he places Joyce's experiments in the context of similar practices to be found in Virginia Woolf, Thomas Wolfe and other novelists. Beja defines the epiphany as a 'sudden spiritual manifestation, whether from some object, scene, event, or memorable phase of the mind – the manifestation being out of proportion to the significance on strictly logical relevance of whatever produces it.'[8] Beja rightly stresses the apparent triviality of the trigger to the epiphany but his term 'spiritual' (which he actually revises during his discussion of *A Portrait*) raises a serious issue. Are we to take 'epiphany' as an entirely secularised expression of discovery or are we to take it as signalling a transcendental move beyond its trigger to a different dimension of experience? On the whole, Joyce critics seem to incline towards the former but it is certainly the case that the term 'epiphany' has raised many problems of meaning. Robert Scholes addresses these during a running controversy with Florence L. Walzl and draws necessary distinctions between the concept, the process and the literary work.[9] Certainly, the notion of epiphany has proved useful for explaining the organisation of *A Portrait* around pivotal scenes and the novel's implicit incremental progression; and it continues to be applied productively. Richard M. Kain, for instance, shows how selectively Dublin features in *A Portrait* and concludes that 'the environment is more important as a setting or source of epiphany than as a scene for action'.[10]

The fact that Stephen defines 'epiphany' in *Stephen Hero* places this notion within the broader context of his statements on aesthetics, statements which have provoked a minor critical industry in their own right. Early readings examined the truth or falsity of Stephen's theorising, whereas from the 1950s onwards more attention has been paid to the role of his theories in Stephen's development. So James R. Baker (1950–1) declares that it is well-nigh impossible to discuss them in isolation because they represent 'the climax of the young artist's intellectual struggle'.[11] Ellsworth Mason ('Joyce's categories', 1953) was even less impressed and he dismisses Stephen's three aesthetic categories as 'the attempt of a very cocky young man to establish the extreme limits of his ambition'. In other words the question of theory shades yet again into the issue of perspective, ironic or otherwise.[12]

The identification of influence has, of course, played an

important part in Joyce criticism, understandably so given his astonishingly broad area of allusion, and Stephen's theories have been no exception. They have been traced back respectively to Aquinas (William T. Noon), St Augustine (J. Mitchell Morse), Ibsen (Haskell M. Block) and Bergson (Shiv K. Kumar).[13] Kumar's discussion has the interest of positing an influence which cannot easily be assimilated into autobiographical readings of Stephen Dedalus. Most of these exercises in source-spotting attempt to set up approximately parallel correspondences between Stephen's theories and the 'original'. Maurice Beebe's 'Joyce and Aquinas' (1957), however, intelligently diverts from the pattern in order to show that 'Joyce follows the form of certain scholastic principles, but by denying the premises upon which they are based, distorts the meaning'.[14] Just as Beebe shows how Stephen exploits scholasticism for his own ends, S. L. Goldberg (1961) firmly directs the reader to consider the implications of Stephen's theories (which for him derive most conspicuously from Shelley) for his own development. Pointing out the drawbacks of these theories, he declares: 'Stephen is intent on the dissociation of art and life, on the autonomy and integrity of the work of art in itself.'[15] Joyce's critics have in general tried to negotiate a careful path between recognising the dramatic status of Stephen's pronouncements and acknowledging their relevance to the novel as a whole.

An unusual diversion from the main current of criticism has been John B. Smith's *Imagery and the Mind of Stephen Dedalus* (1980), which attempts to inject new rigour into the old-fashioned practice of charting out imagery. His main argument – and few would disagree with it – is that 'the dynamic patterns of association among images on the page reflect the developing structure of Stephen's mind.' Smith has applied a method of computer scanning to locate the clusters of images which occur in each chapter of *A Portrait* and, although he has interesting points to make about the processes of Stephen's perceptions, there are a number of problems in his approach. Firstly, there is the question of the central term: an image is defined as 'any word or phrase with a sensuous or thematic aspect'. Leaving aside the difficulty of where thematic significance stops and sensuous appeal begins, 'image' carries very strong connotations of the visual. Secondly, a computer scan could presumably only show recurrence and conjunction but not relation, and so would be valuable basically for indicating word-frequency. And lastly, the theme of fear could be alluded to without the word as such appearing at all. Indeed, recurring terms in *A Portrait* have a disconcerting habit of shifting from one context to another. For these and other reasons Smith's attempts to quantify the novel's imagery remain less than convincing.

Of recent years Joyce criticism has developed in three main areas: post-structuralism, Joyce's cultural context and feminist criticism. The earliest and most prominent post-structuralist reading of Joyce must be Colin MacCabe's *James Joyce and the Revolution of the Word* (1978), which applies Lacan in order to question our habits of reading. MacCabe's basic premise is that, unlike realistic fiction, 'Joyce's texts ... lack any final and privileged discourse within them which dominates the others through its claim of access to the real.' In common with other Joyce critics he finds a confusion in *Stephen Hero* between the protagonist's discourse and the impersonal narration, whereas *A Portrait* assembles a 'montage of discourses' and 'refuses to tell us stories'.[16] The novel actually levels a deconstructive tendency against the efforts of Stephen's father (and, one could add, the other male authority-figures) who try to fix the young man's identity. MacCabe has been rightly taken to task by David Lodge for greatly oversimplifying the procedures of the realistic novel where free indirect speech enables the novelist to move between mimesis and diegesis which are two basic poles of possibility in all fiction.[17] MacCabe also seems to imply a levelling out of discourse in Joyce's fiction which again does not fit the facts. Joyce was well aware that political and institutional power resides to an important extent in a command of language and therefore dramatises repeated clashes between discourses.

MacCabe's interpretation of *A Portrait* carries implications both for gender and for politics which lie beyond the scope of his study although they have been picked up in a pair of articles by Maud Ellmann on the connections between paternity and naming. Her insistence on identity as process is obviously faithful to the method of *A Portrait* which makes a positive fetish out of avoiding fixity, and she has provocative points to make on the disassembly which takes place in the narrative. Drawing comparisons with Wordsworth's *Prelude*, 'Disremembering Dedalus' demonstrates that memory is constantly collapsing and Ellmann declares: 'But the text does not halt at mere dismemberment. The face, the gaze, the footstep and the voice degenerate into images and echoes of themselves.'[18] Ellmann argues strenuously that *A Portrait* is not concerned with representation and thus confirms in the most startling way that it has moved well away from realism. In her 1982 essay 'Poltropic man' she continues this argument to show that identity in *A Portrait* 'develops into a complex circulation of the word and flesh'.[19] Ellmann's essays, clogged by the word-play that seems compulsory to some post-structuralists, pursue suggestive approaches quite congenial to that of Hélène Cixous, who has argued recently that Joyce sets up symbolic networks to give an 'effect of mastery' only to subvert them.[20] Gesturing constantly towards signification, he actually demonstrates the enigmatic nature of the signifying process itself.

The readings just outlined deconstruct the text of *A Portrait* with the effect of producing a result similar to two other recent studies of Joyce, although the latter follow quite different methodologies. Charles Rossman's 1982 essay, 'The reader's role in *A Portrait of the Artist as a Young Man*', attempts a balancing act between two contradictory truths about literature: 'that the text is determinate *and* that the reader is constitutive of meaning'. Having one eye on Wolfgang Iser's analysis of *Ulysses* in *The Implied Reader*, Rossman declares: 'A special difficulty for readers of *A Portrait* is the discovery of an adequate interpretive context for a given epiphanic moment, scene, or episode'.[21] Repeating the by now familiar argument about the novel's expansive progression, Rossman comes to the conclusion that interpretative finality is impossible partly because Joyce retains unexplained factual details which induce uncertainty. Here Rossman anticipates Philip F. Herring's study, *Joyce's Uncertainty Principle* (1987), where he locates a duplicitous tactic on Joyce's part of simultaneously inviting the reader towards 'true' interpretations of his texts and at the same time omitting the key scene or information which would confirm those interpretations. Herring scarcely mentions *A Portrait*, but his identification of a 'seemingly contradictory strategy of producing both ambiguous texts and the keys to interpreting them' has clear implications for the novel.[22] Like the post-structuralist readings, Herring's approach to Joyce destabilises the text, rendering it as an area of conflicting procedures which can scarcely be reconciled in 'static' interpretations.

The more Joyce criticism has tended to concentrate on the rhetorical techniques of his works the more their context has been ignored. Dominic Manganiello sets out to refute the image of Joyce as an ivory tower aesthete in his 1980 study *Joyce's Politics* which demonstrates in exhaustive detail the surprising extent of his political interests. Particularly valuable to any study of *A Portrait* is his documentation of Joyce's involvement in the Irish literary movement and his initial support for Sinn Fein. Joyce followed the nationalist journals closely and accepted their view of Britain as an occupying power together with Ireland's need for economic self-assertion, although it is doubtful whether his scheme of exporting tweeds to Trieste would have significantly boosted the national economy. He recoiled from the cause of Sinn Fein in the face of their puritanism, literary prescription and evident antisemitism; all of which he resolutely countered in *Ulysses*. Where Manganiello produces an intellectual biography, Cheryl Herr (in *Joyce's Anatomy of Culture*, 1986) carries off interpretations of an altogether higher calibre. Herr's focus lies on the 'impress' of social history on Joyce's fiction, but instead of setting up crude sets of correspondence or simply glossing those scenes in the fiction with social implications, she argues that Joyce possessed a shrewd awareness of the cultural forms surrounding him: 'When Joyce uses the format of a newspaper, a play, a playbill, a song, or a sermon he foregrounds the repetitive nature of institutional messages, for those passages in his fiction direct attention to the strictly conventional packaging of experience by institutions.'[23] In other words, Joyce senses the discourses of his culture – as Herr puts it, 'in Joyce's fiction, all power is discursive' – and repeatedly exposes the intertextual nature of his narratives. This makes a major step forward in criticism of *A Portrait*, as well as of *Ulysses* which offers plenty of obvious grist to Herr's mill, because it raises questions about the novel's rhetorical evocation of its own context.

In 1982 a collection of essays edited by Suzette Henke and Elaine Unkeless, *Women in Joyce*, was published, which marked the beginning of substantial feminist readings of Joyce's works. Henke supplies an excellent close discussion of female figures in *A Portrait* who collectively constitute a psychological 'other' to the predominently male perspectives. Henke's forceful analysis of the psychodynamics of Stephen's shifting attitude to women will be used later in this study and it is unusual in feminist readings of Joyce for its close and exclusive attention to a specific text. Bonnie Kime Scott's *Joyce and Feminism* (1984) is a frankly revisionist work in attempting to complement the Ellmann biography by showing what an important part was played in the writer's life by figures like Maud Gonne, Constance Markewicz and of course Nora Barnacle (as of 1988 the subject of a biography in her own right). One of the most interesting areas of discussion in Scott is her demonstration that Irish nationalism was a 'liberating case for young women'. Joyce was well aware of this through his friend Francis Skeffington and demonstrated his awareness in the character of Emma Clery, who 'offers a field of resistances in style, character, and the critical interpretations she has received, richer and broader than that for most of Joyce's woman characters.'[24] Where Scott's first book deals in character or historical individuals, her next analysis, *James Joyce* (1987), concentrates on the role of gender within styles of expression. She stresses Stephen's 'acquisition of academic male discourse from the classical and theological education provided by the Jesuits' and has valuable points to make too about Simon Dedalus' rhetorical tactics in the Christmas Dinner scene, all of which are guaranteed to keep the women in a subsidiary role.[25] Here again this volume has comparatively little to say about *A Portrait* but Scott opens up a fruitful line of discussion by asking how gender is involved in the power-politics of discourse. A special number of *Modern Fiction Studies* (35, 3, (1989)) has been devoted to feminist readings of Joyce but includes hardly any material on *A Portrait*.

Theoretical Perspectives

Theoretical approaches to *A Portrait* have tended to concentrate in five main areas. The novel's symbolism has been demonstrated in considerable detail by close analyses of motifs which still have the cumulative value of demonstrating how astonishingly closely woven is the verbal texture. The fact that *A Portrait* appropriates some of its symbolism from the Catholic Church ironically reveals Joyce's debt to the very institution he rebelled against. Secondly, many critics have attempted with varying degrees of success to apply Stephen's aesthetic pronouncements as his aesthetic performance in the villanelle to the novel as a whole. These attempts have derived Stephen's theories from a bewildering variety of sources and have never coped adequately with the problems of voice and perspective which arise here. It is obvious, for instance, that Joyce renders Stephen's theorising ironically as a series of postures which can scarcely be used to explain their own undermining. The structure of the novel received one of its earliest and still most cogent accounts by Hugh Kenner as a complex series of repetitions and contrasts, but more recently post-structuralists have brought the stability of the novel's discourse into question, arguing that the text is shifting and elusive. The final two approaches of recent years also extend our awareness of the novel in offering historicist accounts of the cultural discourses which traverse the novel and in foregrounding the issue of gender.

A common factor in a number of these approaches has been an emphasis on the novel's discourse, on the way it assembles a series of contrasting voices. In 1905 Joyce wrote to his brother Stanislaus: 'The struggle against conventions in which I am at present involved was not entered into by me so much as a protest against these conventions as with the intention of living in conformity with my moral nature.'[1] The opposition Joyce identifies between the individual and convention lies at the heart of *A Portrait*, which he was just beginning when he made the quoted statement, and a crucial critical task is to explore the rhetorical nature of this opposition. The theorist whose work opens up new avenues of discussion here is the Russian critic Mikhail Bakhtin, whose notion of dialogics can help to explain both the internal and external oppositions of Joyce's novel. In what follows I offer a summary of Bakhtin's general theories which will then be applied in detail to the different sections of *A Portrait*.

Bakhtin's premise from which he develops his theory of dialogics is that discourse is a social phenomenon. The relation of the speaker to her/his utterance becomes a complex one since that utterance occurs within a larger sequence of social and historical changes taking place within the language as a whole. Tzvetan Todorov quotes a 1974 fragment by Bakhtin which declares:

> There is no first or last discourse, and dialogical context knows no limits (it disappears into an unlimited past and in our unlimited future). Even *past* meanings, that is those that have arisen in the dialogue of past centuries, can never be stable (completed once and for all, finished), they will always change (renewing themselves) in the course of the dialogue's subsequent development.[2]

Bakhtin denies any utterance a firm beginning or end. Instead, he places his emphasis on continuous process and on the interaction between utterances. This would imply the difficulty or at least the arbitrary nature of closing off a novel since discourse by its very nature is unfinished. Earlier in the century Virginia Woolf had made a similar point about the processes of perception. Including Joyce's *A Portrait* among her examples in her essay 'Modern fiction', she insists on the novelist's freedom to convey a new perceived shape to experience: 'Let us record the atoms as they fall upon the mind in the order in which they fall, let us trace the pattern, however disconnected and incoherent in appearance, which each sight or incident scores upon the consciousness'.[3] Woolf's declaration fails to recognise the role of language in this process and thereby traps the writer – notionally at least – within a single consciousness. This emphasis has bedevilled discussion of stream-of-consciousness and related fiction right up to the present. Dorothy Van Ghent's chapter on *A Portrait*, for instance, in *The English Novel: Form and fiction* (1953) persists in identifying phases of Stephen's consciousness because she does not have the theoretical means of moving between that consciousness and its socio-historical context. Bakhtin, however, shifts our attention away from perception on to language and immediately situates the subject within a pattern of interrelationships. Since language is socially and historically determined, it now becomes impossible to regard thought as the exclusive possession of the individual, and Bakhtin's dialogical approach to language helps to explain how Stephen Dedalus comes into a situation of already existing discourses and then struggles to develop an identity among them.

Although the term 'language' is singular Bakhtin effectively transforms it into a collective notion because, he explains, 'at any given moment of its historical existence, language is heteroglot from top to bottom: it represents the co-existence of socio-ideological contradictions between the present and the past, between differing epochs of the past, between different socio-ideological groups in the present, between tendencies, schools, circles and so forth, all given a bodily form' (*DI*, 291). Instead of being a static unity, language, according to Bakhtin, consists of a ferment of processes where different registers, dialects and sub-languages are encountering each other and striving for primacy. Bakhtin himself is writing dialogically against the notion of a 'unitary language' which he counters with the terms 'heteroglossia' and 'polyglossia'. At stake is the very composition of a culture since what Bakhtin calls the 'centripetal forces in socio-linguistic and ideological life' perform acts of coercion by attempting the 'victory of one reigning language (dialect) over the others, the supplanting of languages, their enslavement, the process of illuminating them with the True Word' (*DI*, 271). Bakhtin charges his expressions with political connotations in order to fix in our minds an association between monoglossia and cultural hegemony, an authoritative single language and political coercion. The relevance of this general principle to the Irish literary situation at the beginning of the century should be obvious. The simple fact that Joyce chose to write a novel about Ireland in English constituted a political act, and the political implications of a country seeking independence but continuing to use the language of its imperial master preoccupied Joyce throughout his career. Any recognition of linguistic diversity, Bakhtin suggests, tugs against an authoritarian pressure within the official culture towards a single discourse, and also demarginalises professional jargons, slang and dialect which might have been suppressed in favour of a 'standard' language.

In arriving at this position Bakhtin proposes dialogue as the basic model of discourse. Predictably, this premise leads him to favour speech over the written language and he recoils from linguistic scholasticism by stressing over and over again the *life* of a language. This vitality is demonstrated through interaction between speakers and works. Accordingly Bakhtin identifies three units: the text, the utterance and the word. Introducing Bakhtin's work to French readers in the 1960s, Julia Kristeva coined the term 'intertextuality' to convey the principles that 'any text is constructed as a mosaic of quotations; any text is the absorption and transformation of another.'[4] These propositions radically revise the general notion of originality and bear a special relevance to Joyce's works in particular. The more research is pursued on his fiction – and the present study will be no exception – the more Joyce's works emerge as a carefully wrought tissue of quotations and allusions. Kristeva's mosaic analogy was used by Joyce himself in connection with the uncorrected galley-proofs of *Ulysses* and was subsequently developed by such critics as A. Walton Litz.[5] The analogy was a tactical one because these critics were in effect warning the reader of Joyce's last two novels not to expect conventional narrative progression but rather to consider the gradual filling out of structural patterns. The text of the *Portrait* is less obviously a mosaic but even here the parallel can fruitfully divert us from the last traces of an autobiographical reading. We should, however, bear in mind that intertextuality involves more than references to other literary works. When he was elaborating on Kristeva's position Roland Barthes stressed that 'bits of codes, formulae, rhythmic models, fragments of social languages, etc. pass into the text and are re-distributed within it, for there is always language before and around the text.' Unlike literary allusions these traces cannot always be identified. Accordingly, 'the intertext is a general field of anonymous formulae whose origin can scarcely ever be located.'[6] We shall see this principle in operation in the *Portrait* as Stephen manoeuvres his way through the various discourses confronting him. In his study of Bakhtin, Todorov declared a preference for the term 'intertextuality' over 'dialogics' as being more precise, but the former hypostasises a relation while the latter has the advantage of denoting a continuing process.

Bakhtin asserted that, like the text, neither the utterance nor the word should be perceived as isolated entities. His essay 'The problem of the text' states: 'an utterance is defined not only by its relation to the object and to the speaking subject–author, but – for us most important of all – by its direct relation to other utterances within the limits of a given sphere of communication' (*SG*, 122). Without ever losing sight of the object of discourse Bakhtin repeatedly insists that that object is always coloured by earlier discourse so that the individual utterance of one point of view engages with earlier expressions of different points of view. This means that there is no such thing as 'pure' discourse; on the other hand it does not follow that Bakhtin's theory dissolves discourse into arbitrary relativism. Discourse, in other words, must be relative to the discourses available at any given historical moment.

A similar situation obtains with the smallest unit of discourse, since 'the word is born in a dialogue as a living rejoinder within it; the word is shaped in dialogic interaction with an alien word that is already in the object. A word forms a concept of its own object in a dialogic way' (*DI*, 279). Bakhtin spatialises the field of discourse as a verbal environment which the individual utterance penetrates. Once again there is no single or simple relation between word and object at a 'particular historical moment'. Willy-nilly the utterance 'cannot fail to become an active participant in social dialogue' (*DI*, 276). Kristeva praises Bakhtin for presenting the word as an 'intersection of textual surfaces' and continues: 'the word's status is ... defined *horizontally* (the word in the text belongs to both writing subject and addressee) as well as *vertically* (the word in the text is oriented towards an anterior or synchronic literary corpus).'[7] The word thus operates simultaneously along two axes, 'dialogue' and 'ambivalence', the latter signifying the interpenetration between discourse and history. Here again Bakhtin's theories bear sharply on *A Portrait*. Many critics have commented in passing on Stephen Dedalus' preoccupation with language, but have tended to interpret this interest as a dandyish sign of his literary inclinations. By noting, for example, the 'infinite gradations in the degree of foreignness (or assimilation) of words' Bakhtin alerts us to the speaker's distance from her/ his discourse (*SG*, 121). Given that the action of *A Portrait* takes place at a time when agitation for home rule was reaching a peak, and given that this agitation partly revolved around the promotion of Irish, Stephen's attempts to situate himself in relation to the imperial language become charged with political implications.

If dialogue is the basic pattern of discourse then each utterance implies a response: 'the word in living conversation is directly, blatantly, oriented toward a future answer-word: it provokes an answer, anticipates it and structures itself in the answer's direction.' Bakhtin then generalises further: 'all rhetorical forms ... are oriented toward the listener and his answer' (*DI*, 280). Transpose this proposition into the field of criticism and we find Bakhtin approaching reception theory. Since a respondent is built into the very nature of rhetoric, then reading becomes a necessary part of the circuit of discourse and Bakhtin nimbly avoids setting the reader apart from the text by arguing that the understanding of dialogical utterances is itself dialogical: 'the person who understands ... becomes a participant in the dialogue' (*SG*, 125). Recently Don H. Bialostosky has identified the reader's response as an integral part of dialogics: 'the author designs characters to provoke articulate responsiveness of one person to another on common human ground. Instead of issuing in non-verbal recognition or feeling an attitude, the unfinalized interplay of value-charged discourse in the dialogic work continues in the diverse verbal responses it provokes in its readers.'[8] Bakhtin did not pursue the implications of such statements, preferring to repeat his central tenet that dialogue is elastic and inclusive, and that it never ends. This was even true for his own writings which repeat and elaborate earlier positions, and in that way build up a coherent œuvre.

Bakhtin reserves pride of place in his writing for the novel as a genre which exploits heteroglossia. He repeatedly contrasts it with poetry, which he tends to dismiss as monological, but Bakhtin can only perform this move by narrowing the range of poetry down to the lyric. In 'Discourse in the novel' Bakhtin appears to use poetry not as a subject in its own right, but rather as a springboard towards identifying the rhetorical characteristics of the novel. Elsewhere he admits poetry into the general dialogical play of discourse:

> Does the author not always stand *outside* the language as material for the work of art? Is not any writer (even the pure lyricist) always a 'dramaturge' in the sense that he directs all words to others' voices, including to the image of the author (and to other authorial masks)? (*SG*, 110)

One implication of this unavoidable detachment is that discourse becomes double-voiced, responding to other discourse which is already present.

The novel genre, according to Bakhtin, is uniquely aware of linguistic diversity. It is a 'hybrid' which recognises the multiple connotations of words; and – even more important – it is multivoiced. This polyphony provides the source of the novel's vitality and it is therefore no surprise that novels repeatedly incorporate concealed forms of others' speech. Bakhtin gives examples from *Little Dorrit* to show what he designates 'pseudo-objective motivation', that is, characters' motivation being masked as narratorial. An author becomes situated among discourses: 'all forms involving a narrator or a posited author signify to one degree or another by their presence the author's freedom from a unitary and singular language, a freedom connected with the relativity of literary and language systems' (*DI*, 314–15). The novelist's comic play with registers, 'character zones' (areas of narrative incorporating the idiolect of that character) and introductory or framing devices relativise language boundaries and draw attention to the materiality of language. Kristeva adds Joyce to Bakhtin's list of examples of polyphony, although *The Waste Land* would fit just as well (Eliot's working title *He Do the Police in Different Voices* gives us a relevant hint).

Ulysses repeatedly shifts its level of discourse so as to deny any single register primacy. In Chapter 12 Joyce repeatedly juxtaposes the colloquial idiom of the local narrator with passages of grotesquely inflated epic grandeur so as to mock the literary tones associated with writers like William Sharp or the Young Ireland movement. The chapter concludes with a rhetorical bathos which contrasts facetiously with the figure of ascension. Bloom is chased away from the bar by the Citizen's dog:

> And the last we saw was the bloody car rounding the corner and old sheepface on it gesticulating and the bloody mongrel after it with his lugs back for all he was bloody well worth to tear him limb from limb. Hundred to five! Jesus, he took the value of it out of him, I promise you.
>
> When, lo, there came about them all a great brightness and they beheld the chariot wherein He stood ascend to heaven. And they beheld Him in the chariot, clothed upon in the glory of the brightness, having raiment as of the sun, fair as the moon and terrible that for awe they durst not look upon Him. And there came a voice out of heaven, calling: Elijah! Elijah! And He answered with a main cry: Abba! Adonai! And they beheld Him even Him, ben Bloom Elijah, amid clouds of angels ascend to the glory of the brightness at an angle of fortyfive degrees over Donohoe's in Little Green Street like a shot off a shovel. (*U*, 282–3)

The passage shifts abruptly from a spoken idiom with profane modifiers which appeals to a collective enjoyment of the spectacle, to a biblical register which suddenly reclassifies Bloom as a transfigured national leader. As 'we' gives way to 'they' Joyce superscribes this ascension over the biblical narrative in 2 Kings 2.xi: 'And it came to pass, as they still went on, and talked, that, behold, there appeared a chariot of fire, and parted them both asunder; and Elijah went up by a whirlwind into heaven.' Joyce conflates the story of Elijah with the spirit of Christ (through a half-quotation from Galatians 4.vi) to counteract the antisemitic hostility towards Bloom. By repeating formulae out of context ('lo', 'and they beheld', etc.) Joyce foregrounds them as verbal devices and then, just as he has established a pastiche solemnity, he allows the passage to collapse back to the prosaic by incorporating incongruous topographical details and an analogy more appropriate to the preceding colloquial idiom. Bloom as a character is refracted through different styles and the main event at this point in the novel is not so much Bloom's treatment as the comic collision between two starkly opposed stylistic registers.

We shall see in a moment the special value Bakhtin attaches to comedy. First we need to recognise how well dialogical theory explains the volatile nature of the novel's text. Bakhtin was sketching out a programme for a new stylistics in direct opposition to an approach which viewed the literary work as a 'hermetic and self-sufficient whole': 'Should we imagine the work as a rejoinder in a given dialogue, whose style is determined by its interrelationship with other rejoinders in the same dialogue ... then traditional stylistics does not offer an adequate means for approaching such a dialogized style' (*DI*, 274). It is precisely in areas like polemics and parody that Bakhtin suggests dialogics can bring new light, and in *Problems of Dostoevsky's Poetics* he argues at length that the Russian depicts a pluralistic world and characteristically replaces sequence with contrasts within a present moment. Dostoevsky's characters are virtual dialogicians in anticipating responses; the narrator of *Notes from Underground*, for instance, polemicises everything but leaves a 'loophole of consciousness', in other words the 'retention for oneself of the possibility for altering the ultimate, final meaning of one's own words'. Since the 'expressive form' of Dostoevsky's society had fallen apart he constantly homed in on the 'highly intense struggle of *I* and *other* in every external manifestation of a person'.[9]

Joyce's world too was breaking apart into disparate languages, and the contrast which Bakhtin draws between Tolstoy and Dostoevsky is helpful in explaining an all-important change of method from *Stephen Hero* to *A Portrait*. For Bakhtin Tolstoy's propagandising impulse leads him to use his narrators to question the reader's presumptions about value, whereas Dostoevsky places utterance against utterance to avoid any suggestion of cultural homogeneity. The analogy with Joyce at this point is approximate but nevertheless useful. In *Stephen Hero* the protagonist's actions are referred to an overriding satirical narrative voice which stands ironically apart from the novel's characters and from Stephen himself. *A Portrait*, in spite of its title, establishes a vocal diversity by attenuating the narrative voice into a verbal ground against which Stephen's expressive resources can reveal themselves at any one point. It now becomes essential to speak of styles and voices in the plural. What Dostoevsky's characters say, according to Bakhtin, 'constitutes an arena of never-ending struggle with others' words, in all realms of life and creative ideological activity' (*DI*, 349). Exactly the same is true of *A Portrait*, where Stephen's discourse opposes those of his surrounding culture and even internalises this struggle as a clash between rival voices within his psyche.

Bakhtin's discussion questions the notion of a speaker originating discourse. Since language in all its heterogeneity precedes the individual, it now becomes more appropriate to talk of *transmitting* discourse, and Bakhtin notes three devices used by the novel towards this end: hybridisation, stylisation and variation. The first of these involves the 'mixture of two social languages within the limits of a single utterance', where the novel uses one language to shed light on another (*DI*, 358). The quotation from *Ulysses* given above does this, comically estranging the reader from the discourse. And Bakhtin argues that the evocation of this 'otherness' in language is one of the main purposes of the novel: namely, to encourage the 'process of coming to know one's own language as it is perceived in someone else's language' (*DI*, 365). Not only does Stephen Dedalus quote the words of others far more than he admits, but he also experiences an alienation from his own language so severe that it questions his relation to Anglo-Irish culture.

At this point we need to turn to Bakhtin's discussion of the carnivalesque to see what function comedy possesses within dialogics. *Rabelais and his World* attempts to open up an area for critical consideration which will counter the neglect of comedy. Just as in the carnival laughter reasserted itself after official exclusion, so Bakhtin sets out to record a Menippean tradition of comic fiction which grew out of the collective folk consciousness. During the carnival hierarchical modes of speech and behaviour were suspended and Bakhtin finds a continuation of these procedures in works like *Gargantua and Pantagruel* or *Don Quixote*. These novels are polyphonic, but specifically they use different registers to attack the discourses of officialdom. The latter are unmasked and destroyed as 'something false, hypocritical, greedy, limited, narrowly rationalistic, inadequate to reality.'[10] Parody clearly becomes crucial in this context and what Bakhtin calls an 'unresolved conversation' is set up between the new work and the language being parodied. The contrasts between up and down are precise here, downwards being the direction towards the world and the physical correlative of bathos and degradation. Bakhtin examines Rabelais' bodily imagery partly as a reminder of human mortality and, of course, as a means of undermining human dignity. Julia Kristeva brings out the subversive nature of this writing: 'the carnival challenges God, authority and social law; in so far as it is dialogical, it is rebellious.'[11]

The first casualty in carnivalesque comedy must be literary solemnity and we have seen an example in the concluding passage from the 'Cyclops' episode of how *Ulysses* juxtaposes high and low styles. Joyce's pastiche of the Bible is irreverent in denying that work any ultimate textual authority and he uses the pastiche to target Irish hopes of a new messiah. Rabelais' parodies, bathos and bodily references have an immediate and obvious relevance to *Ulysses* and it is surprising that critics have not made more of the parallel.[12] In the case of *A Portrait*, where the parodies are more muted the notion of the carnivalesque sheds light on one specific passage. Stephen is attending a lecture on physics but finds more stimulation from the comments of other students than from the lecture itself:

> His fellow student's rude humour ran like a gust through the cloister of Stephen's mind, shaking into gay life limp priestly vestments that hung upon the walls, setting them to sway and caper in a sabbath of misrule. The forms of the community emerged from the gustblown vestments, the dean of studies, the portly florid bursar with his cap of grey hair, the president, the little priest with feathery hair who wrote devout verses, the squat peasant form of the professor of economics, the tall form of the young professor of mental science discussing on the landing a case of conscience with his class like a giraffe cropping high leafage among a herd of antelopes, the grave troubled prefect of the sodality, the plump roundheaded professor of Italian with his rogue's eyes. They came ambling and stumbling, tumbling and capering, kilting their gowns for leap frog, holding one another back, shaken with deep false laughter, smacking one another behind and laughing at their rude malice, calling to one another by familiar nicknames, protesting with sudden dignity at some rough usage, whispering two and two behind their hands. (*P*, 196–7)

Stephen's fantasy image emerges from the clash between the decorum of the event and the irreverent remarks of the other students. The latter act like a catalyst and populate the space of Stephen's imagination which ironically resembles the very monasticism he is ostensibly rejecting. The passage contrasts life with death, physical vigour with the empty clerical robes; and then orchestrates Stephen's instructors in a dance with its own rhythms. The Rabelaisian reduction to the physical is glimpsed in the comparison of moral debate to a 'giraffe cropping high leafage among a herd of antelopes' and rank (and decorum) are suspended as the clerics caper in play. This is a local image completely detached from the church calendar which would link the feast of misrule with the Christmas season, and, because it is entirely internalised, constitutes a private mental act of rebellion against the dull routine of scholarly learning. This is, however, an isolated instance in *A Portrait*. For a sustained orchestration of comic irreverence we have to wait until *Ulysses*, as David Fuller has shown in his companion study within the present series. The main area of Bakhtin's work relevant to *A Portrait* remains his writing on dialogics since this helps to explain the textual dynamics of that novel so successfully.

The most sustained attempt to apply Bakhtin's theories to Joyce has been R. B. Kershner's *Joyce, Bakhtin, and Popular Literature* (1989). As more information emerges about the omnivorous nature of Joyce's reading Kershner has turned to Bakhtin for theoretical help in substantiating a general position that 'Joyce's characters speak themselves into existence, are seduced, appeased, threatened, annoyed, and shaped by the languages around them' (K, 20). Although he rightly states that *Ulysses* and *Finnegan's Wake* would lend themselves to Bakhtinian analysis, he turns his attention primarily to *Dubliners* and *A Portrait*. Broadly speaking, Kershner's study covers two overlapping areas. On the one hand he examines the use of other works which supply 'ghost narratives' to Joyce's own fictions; and on the other he analyses the dialogical internal nature of Joyce's narratives. Bakhtin allows Kershner to develop the truism that *A Portrait* traces out growth by placing language at the centre of this process. The problem of consciousness is 'having to choose a language' and the psyche in this account becomes a social space to be filled with ideological signs (*DI*, 295). Kershner argues that 'Stephen is a product of his listening and reading, an irrational sum of the texts, written and spoken, to which he has been exposed', and he demonstrates this through a particularly fine account of Stephen's schooldays which deserves detailed attention at the appropriate place (K, 162). Kershner returns again and again to the variety of voices in *Dubliners* and *A Portrait*, and in both cases shows that characters engage dynamically with the discourses of their environment.

The bulk of Kershner's writing on the *Portrait* consists of a discussion of those works which collectively supply an 'ambiguous countertext to the novel as a whole' (K, 152). These fall into four main categories. In the first Kershner discusses schoolboy fiction like *Tom Brown's Schooldays* or Frederick Farrar's *Eric* (1858). Repeating the differences between Stephen's experiences and those of Joyce himself pointed out in Bruce Bradley's study *James Joyce's Schooldays* (1982), Kershner concludes that Stephen was composed as Tom Brown's 'antitype' in wilfully standing apart from physical activities like football and cricket. Kershner then continues: 'Stephen's idea of selfhood is shaped by his reading, and to a far greater extent than he recognizes by his *early* reading' (K, 189–90). He shows that romances like *The Count Of Monte Cristo* introduce the glamour of exile (and, he might have added, increases Stephen's sense of himself as a wronged victim); and that Stephen's schoolbooks like Peter Parley's tales offer him narratives which he can re-enact when he goes to see the rector of Clongowes. Kershner's final category of texts is those either reviewed or possessed by Joyce. Thus he notes that Havelock Ellis's *The New Spirit* (1890) almost certainly supplied the themes exploited in Stephen's intellectual development, namely anti-institutionalism, his respect for Ibsen and his idealisation of art. Edward Dujardin's *L'Initiation au péché et à l'amour* (1898) rather than his better known *Les Lauriers sont coupés* offered Joyce a possible structural model in its discontinuous scenic sequence. Kershner's texts are chosen selectively and his basic discussion of intertextuality never really allows the full implications of Bakhtin's dialogics to emerge. Nevertheless, he does supply yet more examples of Joyce's general allusiveness and by so doing helps to disqualify a naive autobiographical reading of *A Portrait*. Stanislaus Joyce's words cannot be repeated too often: '*A Portrait of the Artist* is not an autobiography; it is an artistic creation.'[13]

II

A Portrait of the Artist as a Young Man: A Reading of the Text

1

Stephen Dedalus' Schooldays

'Consciousness awakens to independent ideological life precisely in a world of alien discourses surrounding it, and from which it cannot initially separate itself' (*DI*, 345). Bakhtin's explanation of the social origins of identity stresses a multiplicity of voices which is established right from the beginning of *A Portrait*. Its opening 'moocow' narrative is only briefly single-voiced. The second paragraph introduces a diegetic shift which evokes a situation of narrating and which identifies Stephen's father as the narrator and Stephen himself as the addressee of the narrative. This situation rapidly fills with more voices (Mrs Dedalus', Dante's), but a keynote for the whole novel is struck by the identification of utterance with male authority. Even the prediction of punishment by Dante confirms this identification because, as we learn later in the chapter, she prides herself on speaking with the voice of the Catholic Church.

Story-telling is scarcely introduced before Joyce demonstrates Stephen's capacity to appropriate stories imaginatively by casting himself as the protagonist. He becomes the boy called 'baby tuckoo' just as he later becomes the white-clad marshal in his dream at Clongowes, and, even later, as he dramatically enacts the role of Satan in a private drama of spiritual defiance. Stephen unconsciously recognises the simultaneous possibilities of being performer and audience, both of which are stressed in the opening narrative segment, and this recognition involves an as yet unformulated sense of dialectic between the self and the other. Thus, although the segment introduces us to Stephen, it frames his burgeoning thoughts between two passages of external discourse. The 'pull out his eyes' rhyme was given an identificatory tag in its original form as an epiphany ('Joyce to himself'), but in the novel it has no originator, standing as a verse elaboration of Dante's warning. For this reason R. B. Kershner has shrewdly suggested that the rhyme 'serves as a metonym for alien language' (K, 155). The first page of the novel establishes a typographical convention of rendering song or poetry in italics but this rhyme eludes that distinction and is given no originator. It consists of lines in a void and by noting its quality of otherness Kershner implicitly establishes a theme which will recur throughout *A Portrait*: Stephen will be confronted with a whole range of discourses, each one of which will appear alien so that by the end of the novel even at the height of his verbal powers Stephen will have no discourse he can truly call his own.

When the novel takes us on to Stephen's schooldays an alternation is set up initially between a hostile present and more desirable alternatives. The college is cold and damp; home will be warm and cosy. Even when these oppositions reverse or become further modified the basic rhetorical figure remains one of contrast which simplifies down to paired terms: 'term, vacation; tunnel, out; noise, stop' (*P*, 17). Such oppositions derive partly from the highly structured organisation of Clongowes which penetrates Stephen's imagination as a system of competing groups (the white rose and red rose teams of the mathematics class, the higher and lower lines, etc.) or of contrasting voices. Stephen anticipates the argument at the Christmas dinner table in his conviction that, whatever 'politics' may mean, it has 'two sides'; and the 'cries' of the prefect of studies contrast with Father Arnall's voice after the pandying which becomes 'very gentle and soft'. Even Stephen's dreams are structured around opposites. His fantasy of the silent ghost of a murderer (a

46

kind of anti-self) gives way to a collective and vocalised dream of going home for the holidays. At this stage in the novel the narrative discourse stresses Stephen's perceptions of similarity ('and') and difference. Characteristically, 'but' signals a limitation in his understanding, a disparity which he cannot explain.

For much of Chapter 1 Stephen appears to be silent and passive but the rhetorical means of recording his thoughts suggests on the contrary that his mind is very active, particularly in manoeuvring his way through the statements of others. Kershner is right that 'his mind buzzes with borrowed expressions, languages that he tries on like suits of clothing; but unlike his grey-belted suit he cannot discard them at will' (K, 157). It is certainly true that if Stephen does not understand a word he resorts to repetition as a minimal application of that word, but Kershner tends to understate the urgency of Stephen's internal dialogue because it is here that the true process of his education takes place. Not only his teachers but every character with whom Stephen has contact is placed in an instructive relation to him. His mother teaches him verbal decorum, Dante explains geography, Athy tests him on his capacity to answer riddles; and the latter case foregrounds the puzzling enigmatic quality of Stephen's experience at Clongowes.

Throughout this chapter knowledge is tied to questions of authority and it is therefore symbolically appropriate that the biggest intellectual mystery confronting Stephen should be the name and identity of God. Again and again Joyce renders the utterances of the prefects and boys at Clongowes as non-specific voices articulating collective points of view or collective authority, and Stephen's passages of thought use these voices as reference points. The following are characteristic formulations:

1. The fellows said it was made of whalebone and leather with lead inside: and he wondered what the pain was like. (P, 46).

2. And the rector would declare that he had been wrongly punished because the senate and the Roman people always declared that the men who did that had been wrongly punished. (*P*, 54–5).

These could not be read as examples of what Bakhtin terms 'pseudo-objective motivation' because he explains the latter as a form 'for concealing another's speech' (*DI*, 305), whereas Joyce repeats this rhetorical pattern so often in Chapter 1 that it emerges as a kind of mental quotation. The first example gives a statement followed by a speculation; even here Stephen is participating in a kind of dialogue by asking himself a silent question. The second example embeds clause within clause ('would declare that . . . always declared that . . .') just as it expresses a quotation from a classical historian like Livy within a quotation from another boy's words. The classical text authorises the 'rebellion' which the boys dream of mounting and the boys' words more significantly authorise Stephen's individual act in going to see the rector.

It would accordingly be a mistake to extrapolate from the physical detail of Stephen standing apart from the boys playing football (our first image of him at Clongowes) that he detaches himself from the ethos and activities of the college. On the contrary, he assimilates the words of those around him to articulate his own thoughts. In that respect the novel confirms V. N. Voloshinov's assertion that inner speech is dialogical. In trying to take a decision, he argues, a debate is set up:

> We argue with ourselves, we try to convince ourselves of the rightness of one decision. Our consciousness seems to be divided into two independent and contradictory voices . . . . *And one of these voices always, independently of our will or consciousness, merges with the point of view, opinions and judgements of the class to which we belong.* (Voloshinov's emphasis)[1]

If for Voloshinov's 'class' we substitute 'social peers' then we have an explanation of how Stephen's mental processes work. His weightiest decision in Chapter 1 – whether or not to go to the rector about his punishment – is articulated as a conflict between the two bodies of authority within his immediate environment: the collective opinion of the boys ('every fellow had said that it was unfair') and the status of his Jesuit instructors. But even on the smallest scale Stephen regularly appropriates the words of others into his consciousness in order to struggle towards understanding. We shall see an even more dramatic instance of essentially the same process at work in the retreat section of *A Portrait*.

A recognition of Stephen's tacit imaginative dependence on the words of others means that we should beware of putting a sharp demarcation between passages of speech and passages of thought. The one can shade easily into the other. Immediately after the Christmas-dinner scene we witness Stephen standing silently in a group which is discussing the truancy of some other boys. Although the immediate issue is one of disobedience, the dialogue revolves around knowledge, around who can explain the boys' wrongdoing. The group divides into an audience which expresses a desire for information and a number of individuals who satisfy that desire, but not without elaborate demonstrations of reluctance. When Wells declares that the boys had drunk the wine in the sacristy Stephen is as shocked as his companions but silently continues the dialogue: 'The fellows all were silent. Stephen stood among them, afraid to speak, listening . . . . How could they have done that?' (*P*, 42). Stephen's silence is not simply shyness but rather a response to the boys' violation of the sacristy. By not speaking Stephen implicitly obeys the rule of spiritual decorum associated with that place, while within his thoughts he continues to participate in the group dialogue.

The two most vivid scenes in Chapter 1 which frame the episode just discussed – the Christmas dinner and the pandying – enact questioning of the pieties of home, country and religion, and of school discipline. We should note that this takes place *vocally*. The heated argument between Dante and the men refers to and verges on physical violence; and the prefect of studies' authoritarian exclamations and orders demonstrate a verbal violence which precedes physical chastisement. Even when Stephen does not participate orally, absorbing the utterances of others, his mental dynamics, accelerated by the two events just described, reveal a tentative attempt to negotiate between rival possibilities. Handicapped by a naive assumption that answers must be either right or wrong, Stephen does nevertheless internalise the principle of dialogue that one discourse will encounter another. Bakhtin pushes this principle towards the oral by asserting baldly that the 'fundamental condition' of a novel, its defining nature, 'is the *speaking person and his discourse*' (*DI*, 332: his emphasis). This definition narrowly excludes written discourse which should figure within Bakhtin's general notion of heteroglossia, but it does help to bring out the multivocal nature of *A Portrait*.

The first time that voice dramatically clashes with voice is the famous Christmas-dinner scene. Pivotal in swinging Stephen's attitude towards the Catholic clergy away from respect, this scene depicts a complex series of speech acts which have only recently been analysed by Michael Toolan. He shrewdly points to the number of challenging moves which occur in the dialogue despite the veneer of politeness dictated by the 'festive' season. Toolan documents in detail how Dante gives as good as she gets and explains: 'from a socio-cultural perspective there is an unexpected vehemence in much of Dante's talk, an unexpected frequency in the number of conversational turns she takes and a noticeable refusal to suffer the men's options in silence.'[2] Toolan's emphasis falls on the tactics of dialogue but it is also important in this scene to note an increasing clash between different idioms. While Simon Dedalus and Mr Casey use idiom and colloquialism to appeal to a tacit agreement between male cronies (the former particularly uses redundant expressions to signal a mood of vague geniality), Dante speaks in direct absolute assertions ('it is religion'). In a sense, she takes it upon herself to speak with the authority of the Church, supporting her statements with biblical quotation and referring to the clergy as a collective entity. The two men, however, use historical and personal particularity to attack this status and, as the temperature of the dialogue rises, its terms collapse into a comically stark opposition between the physical and profane ('tub of guts'), and the spiritual ('princes of the church'). Parnell is basically the catalyst for this more general debate on the political standing of the clergy. The scene does not fit a reading where Dante is the helpless victim, for the reasons given above; nor do the oppositions line up according to gender since Mrs Dedalus tries to act as an ineffectual peace-maker.

This episode bears an obvious thematic relevance to questions of nationality, history and religion, but, more strikingly, it demonstrates to Stephen's wondering eyes a radical challenging of authority which anticipates his subsequent sense of injustice after being pandied by the prefect of studies. Looking further ahead into the next chapter the Christmas-dinner scene also anticipates Stephen's futile visit to Cork with his father as the latter attempts to recapture his lost past. The earlier scene alerts us to his father's idiom; the later one develops its gender and dialectal implications since Simon Dedalus and the one old friend he locates trace out a line of patrilinear descent characterised by signs of physical pro-wess. Joyce draws directly on the scene in Shakespeare's *Henry IV* Part 2 where Justice Shallow reflects nostalgically on his youth to parody Simon Dedalus' posturing as a kind of performance. In Cork his companion's repetitive exclamations of 'bedad' are balanced by the former's boozy attempts to defy time ('we're as old as we feel'), whereas in the play Shallow's nostalgia is tempered by a realisation of mankind's common fate: 'Death, as the psalmist saith, is certain to all, all shall die.'[3] Once again

Stephen hardly participates. He is there, not this time as a passive witness, but as a Jamesian 'reflector', helping to establish a distanced and disenchanted perspective on events. His thoughts on the Shelley fragment 'To the moon' which round off this section of Chapter 2 adumbrate a view of human action from beyond the cycle of mortality that strengthens the irony of the allusions to Shakespeare. Stephen recoils from what we shall see is a geographically alien speech register to the secure solitude of print.

In all these scenes Stephen's relation to discourse to a large extent determines how he relates to his social situation. The question of whether or not he belongs at Clongowes depends on his relative willingness to learn the language of the institution and Joyce drew on Thomas Hughes's classic novel to dramatise this issue. His use of *Tom Brown's Schooldays* in *A Portrait* has been recognised by Kershner, who chiefly draws a sharp contrast between Stephen and Tom, and who notes that both Clongowes and Rugby thrive on elitism and on the promotion of sport (K, 168–75). It is, however, more important to pursue the comparison between the two novels since it helps to bring out a general characteristic of *A Portrait*: namely, that each new area of experience for Stephen involves a new discourse. Clongowes is the first substantial context that the novel describes and the institution carries its own jargon. Exactly the same is true in Hughes's novel. When Tom climbs down from the stagecoach at Rugby he is introduced to a bewilderingly new language. His friend-to-be East explains the rules of Rugby football and the narrator glosses the newcomer's reaction: 'Tom's respect increased as he struggled to make out his friend's technicalities, and the other set to work to explain the mysteries of "off your side", "drop-kicks", "punts", "places", and the other intricacies of the great science of football.'[4] The first chapters of Tom's life at Rugby show him asking questions again and again, logically so because at one and the same time he is learning a terminology and a new social structure. Rugby football in that sense functions as a metonym of the working of the school as a whole, appropriately since physical activity is put at a premium. The rules of the game are endlessly repeated in the rules of the lessons, of the school year and of the boys' gradual ascent up the hierarchy of classes. Tom learns the expression 'tossing' only shortly before he has to undergo that initiation ritual and he accelerates his assimilation of Rugby slang because its correct use will identify him as an accepted member of the community. At the beginning of Part 2 of the novel Tom now finds himself in the position occupied earlier by East when he has to instruct another new boy, George Arthur. And so the rhythm of initiation and assimilation will continue with each new arrival.

Superficially, Stephen appears to go through a similar process but its form and implications are more complex than in Hughes's novel. Stephen is asked about his name but is unable to answer. When he is ill Wells (the cause of his illness) questions him about kissing his mother before he goes to bed. When both answers are mocked Stephen uncomfortably tries to merge into the group by participating in their reaction, as it were externalising himself from the ridiculed Stephen: 'They all laughed again. Stephen tried to laugh with them' (*P*, 14). By so doing he dimly recognises the sub-text of the questions which challenge his capacity to participate in the group, but Stephen remains tantalised by the paradox that each alternative answer seems to have been wrong. The difficulty of his predicament becomes further compounded when Athy, his fellow pupil in the infirmary, confronts him with a riddle which he cannot answer. Indeed, Stephen's illness temporarily gives him the luxury of not having to answer such questions, but they continue to haunt his imagination with the unspoken, with areas of expression and meaning which lie beyond his reach.

The relation of slang to the main narrative discourse is also quite different in the two novels. When Stephen notices comic graffiti on the doors of the toilets and we are told: 'some fellow had drawn it there for a cod', the narrator is in effect quoting Stephen repeating a term he has heard from one of the other boys. These terms stand out from their context, whereas the opposite happens in *Tom Brown's Schooldays*. Hughes is describing a representative member of a Wessex family in an attempt to chronicle the imperial vigour of his country. Tom's birthplace signifies his Saxon roots and his education is designed to bring out these racial qualities and fit him to be a ruler of men (the novel is explicitly addressed to a readership of boys). J. Hillis Miller has argued that in adopting a general narrative voice the Victorian novelists were moving 'within the community. They identify themselves with a human awareness which is everywhere at all times within the world of the novel.'[5] This generalisation holds true for Hughes, since his narrator repeatedly assimilates schoolboy slang into his discourse without any jarring of register. The narrator of *Tom Brown's Schooldays* articulates a future composite male voice, as it were the voice of all Rugby graduands (the authorship on the title-page is 'by an old boy'), while the narrator of *A Portrait* retains a detachment from the world of Clongowes. By contrast, we never lose our sense of Stephen's words being inside invisible quotation marks.

The lexicon of slang for Clongowes and Rugby breaks down into three main areas. Firstly, there is the terminology of institutional organisation. Rugby has its praepostor, Clongowes its prefect of studies. Both schools are rigidly hierarchical and it is a fitting symbolic detail that both novels comment on when to use 'sir' in address. Where Hughes describes the fagging system in detail Joyce concentrates on the demarcations between boys of the lower and higher lines. The second area of vocabulary articulates the boys' code of behaviour within which lies a severe taboo against informing on another (Clongowes: 'spying'; Rugby: 'blabbing') as against toadying to one's superiors ('suck' in both books). Joyce's use of this slang is more sophisticated than Hughes's since he brings out a gradation of terminology. Stephen is just old enough to understand 'feck (steal) but not 'smugging', which one of Joyce's commentators has glossed decorously as 'to toy amorously in secret' (G, 99). Finally, this slang encodes understatements of illness ('the collywobbles'), inedible food ('hogwash') and so on. Slang performs a general function in cementing a group and promoting a common mentality. The boys at Clongowes easily extend the expressions of the football pitch into other areas of school life and the authorities formalise this conflict by casting class competitions as the wars of the roses. The one term which Joyce borrows from Hughes and then repeats to the point of parody is 'fellow'. In *Tom Brown's Schooldays* this can become an expression of status (depending on intonation) or a means of distinguishing the schoolboys from the 'louts' (the barbarians beyond the grounds of Rugby). Joyce cuts out these class connotations and focuses his emphasis on the word's denotation of common activity. The use of the word by Stephen enacts its primary meaning, which is to participate in a community, but by the time we reach Chapter 2 such acquiescence to the group has been left behind and the term only lingers on in the mouths of Stephen's teachers and father, the latter evoking a male camaraderie anathema to Stephen. Significantly, 'fellow' resurfaces within the context of Stephen's university circle, this time within a new area of slang which is distinguished from Clongowes by its verbal self-consciousness.

Stephen's willingness to use Clongowes slang demonstrates his participation in the institution, but events bring this relation into question. The climax to Chapter 1 comes in the pandying scene and its sequel. The Christmas-dinner episode shifts abruptly to a discussion by the Clongowes boys which rehearses a series of crimes (theft, sacrilege, sexual misbehaviour) and the justice of the punishment which will ensue. Stephen listens in fascinated silence and then meditates on both, encoding the sacrilege as a 'strange and great sin' which none the less thrills him. By projecting himself into the position of the wrongdoers Stephen takes on their guilt in his imagination and his curiosity about the pandy bat ironically turns out to anticipate his physical beating. Once the prefect of studies appears in the class Stephen to his horror finds himself trapped within a catch-22 logical spiral that since all boys are potential schemers any failure to do class-work becomes a sign of guilt. The prefect's discourse is closed and consists of repeating certain key phrases ('lazy idle loafers'). He participates in a spurious dialogue because he affects to read the tell-tale signs of guilt in boys' features. The responses he expects and receives essentially confirm his suspicions and therefore 'justify' his orders to his hapless victims. The prefect, in other words, enacts his authority by a total domination of the dialogue, whereas the very opposite is true of the rector.

The latter's manner towards Stephen is carefully depicted as a series of courteous responses which tacitly admit Stephen's equality as a participant in the question-and-answer sequence. Stephen explains that he broke his glasses; the rector contemplates him for a moment as if digesting his words and then speaks:

– O well, it was a mistake; I am sure Father Dolan did not know.
– But I told him I broke them, sir, and he pandied me.
– Did you tell him that you had written home for a new pair? the rector asked.
– No, sir.
– O well then, said the rector, Father Dolan did not understand. (*P*, 58–9)

Throughout their exchange the rector demonstrates an open-minded capacity to draw logical inferences (one stylistic sign is his use of an introductory 'well') even if they are at the expense of a member of his staff. This fact in itself, however, does not explain the importance of the episode. Earlier in Chapter 1 a number of occasions occur where Stephen says one thing (what might be convenient at that point) but thinks another. There is an imbalance or disparity between verbal assent and a private dissent within his thoughts. But in the conversation with the rector Stephen harmonises inner feelings and outward expression by insisting quietly on the risk of his being beaten again. The rector's willingness to accept his statements triggers off a wave of new respect in Stephen for the Clongowes authorities which anticipates his renewed acquiescence to the Catholic Church at the end of Chapter 3.

Throughout the opening chapter of *A Portrait* Stephen's shifting commitment to Clongowes is expressed spatially in terms of psychological distance: things seem near or remote. Chapter 2, however, sets up a geographical distance from Stephen's schooldays by locating him variously in Blackrock, Dublin, Belvedere College and Cork. Each location has its own emphasis and, true to one of the novels organisational principles, each discrete section revises the episodes of the preceding chapter. In many ways Stephen becomes distanced from Clongowes. His dramatic encounter with the rector is reduced to comic anecdote by being transferred to his father's voice. Now the adult perspective (the rector's as recounted to Simon Dedalus and then passed on to the family) reverses the child's and drains off the 'heroism' of Stephen's actions. Dedalus senior's skill at mimicry repeats itself in his imitation of the 'mincing nasal tone of the provincial' and, like Mr Casey, Dedalus repeats the punch-line of what has now become a joke at the expense of Stephen's vanity. Just as this revision makes Clongowes seem remote we now witness Stephen mostly outside the classroom, a spatial articulation of his growing detachment from his academic mentors. When one of his teachers accuses him of heresy the occasion carries the dramatic potential of being a reprise of Stephen's confrontation with the prefect of studies. In practice, though, the scene is presented entirely in terms of strategy. Stephen quickly murmurs a revision to his essay which simultaneously demonstrates his knowledge of theology and his detachment from its tenets. 'Murmur' in *A Portrait* is a verb regularly reserved for prayer or the voice of conscience, and it suggests a tone of voice which articulates Stephen's response as much as the actual words he uses. The whole point is, as the teacher recognises, that the words signal a 'submission'.

Stephen's easy escape from his teacher is reversed by his school-fellows, who trap him one evening and try to force him into admitting that Byron was a poor writer because he was a heretic. This encounter transposes the issue of heresy into the field of literature and dramatises the failure of Stephen's attempted role (he forgets his 'silent vows'); whereas later at University College he has perfected a Jesuitical mask. The present event (Stephen being accused by a friend of playing the innocent) triggers off a recall of the literary dispute by the associations of the word 'admit' and by the common presence of punishment with a cane. But the intense pain of Stephen's pandying diminishes in the sequence of events up to the present and indeed a major motif in Chapter 2 is the tendency of Stephen's memories to recede towards unreality.

The fact that his schooldays are drawing to a close is reflected in Stephen's alienation from the exhortatory voices which have been packing his consciousness:

> he had heard about him the constant voices of his father and of his masters, *urging* him to be a gentleman above all things and *urging* him to be a good catholic above all things. These voices had now come to be hollowsounding in his ears. When the gymnasium had been opened he had heard another voice *urging* him to be strong and manly and healthy and when the movement towards national revival had begun to be felt in the college yet another voice had *bidden* him be true to his country and help to raise up her fallen language and tradition. In the profane world, as he foresaw, a wordly voice would *bid* him raise up his father's fallen state by his labours and, meanwhile, the voice of his school comrades *urged* him to be a decent fellow, to shield others from blame or to beg them off and to do his best to get free days for the school. (*P*, 86–7; my emphasis)

Joyce's use of the pluperfect tense pushes these voices into the past, although the retention of the participial form suggests their continuing articulation. The repetition of syntactic pattern, of key verbs like 'urge' and 'bid', and of the central term 'voice' gradually collapses all the injunctions together into a mental noise. The imperatives of Stephen's school join those from other spheres as a collective 'din' which he tries to escape. Temporarily all voices are foregrounded as such in Stephen's consciousness and reduced to a common level of injunction which he tacitly resists without differentiating between them. Past, present and even future voices are dismissed by Stephen as 'hollowsounding', but the novel will demonstrate the dramatic irony in his premature efforts to empty them of substance.

2

The Voices of the Church

Chapter 3 of *A Portrait* opens with Stephen's belly craving for mutton stew and closes with him receiving the host from the ciborium. Between these two extremes of contrasting nourishment the chapter situates other antitheses: the call from the prostitutes and the call of his conscience, isolation against community (and communion), the darkness of night and the brightness of morning, the withered flower of his soul at the beginning and the 'fragrant masses of white flowers' (an emblem of purity) at the end. These contrasts take their place within a tortuous dialectic between body and soul, between Stephen and the Church. The bulk of the chapter traces out the retreat at Belvedere and draws extensively, as critics have shown, on the *Spiritual Exercises* of Ignatius Loyola, specifically on the section dealing with sin. The meditation on Hell contains two preludes:

> First Prelude. The first prelude is a composition of place, which is here to see with the eyes of the imagination the length, breadth, and depth of hell. Second Prelude. To ask for that which I desire. It will be here to ask for an interior sense of the pain which the lost suffer, in order that if through my faults I should forget the love of the eternal Lord, at least the fear of punishment may help me not to fall into sin.[1]

The composition or visualisation of place figures as the first phase in a tripartite sequence, being followed – as this passage indicates – by a petition and finally a 'colloquy' with Christ and with the self, 'to ask what I have done for

Christ'. These preludes (drawn on by Stephen's teachers) introduce an itemised series where each sense in turn is applied to the notion of Hell with the aim of 'making a *colloquy* with Christ our lord' (my emphasis). It is crucial to recognise a system of practice here since Stephen's consciousness has been penetrated by this method of self-analysis even before the retreat gets under way. When wandering round the brothel district Stephen's sense of place is already encoding sensory data according to learnt patterns of moralised imagery – physical squalor suggesting moral pollution and so on. While sitting in his class waiting for the rector, Stephen's realisation of moral guilt once again takes the form of a list, an enumeration of the seven deadly sins introduced by the 'evil seed of lust'.

At one point Joyce typographically stresses Stephen's capacity to incorporate other texts:

> If ever his soul, re-entering her dwelling shyly after the frenzy of his body's lust had spent itself, was turned towards her whose emblem is the morning star, *bright and musical, telling of heaven and infusing peace*, it was when her names were murmured softly by lips whereon there still lingered foul and shameful words, the savour itself of a lewd kiss. (*P*, 108)

The importuning of the prostitutes (outer) and then of the flesh (inner) is referred to as an address to the self which, even within the sentence just quoted, jostles against other voices. The italicised words come from an inspirational address on the Virgin Mary in John Henry Newman's *Discourses Addressed to Mixed Congregations*. Newman, who we should remember is one of Stephen's most cherished stylists, attributes an expressiveness to the Virgin Mary's appearance: 'thy very face and form, sweet Mother, speak to us of the Eternal'; whereas Stephen's sentence dovetails the sacred into the profane so that the deictic reference of the pronouns becomes ambiguous.[2] The sentence carries over echoes of the scene with the prostitute which closes Chapter 2, so that a visit to one dwelling seems to precede an equally functional visit to another. The sentence quoted moves through an arc from the physical to the sacred and back to the physical. On a small scale it looks forward to the Nausicaa section of *Ulysses* where the recitation of the Litany of our Lady of Loreto is inserted into a novelettish account of Bloom's sexual 'encounter' on the beach. The disparity of discourses fractures the perspective on the feminine. In *A Portrait* it remains uncertain whether Stephen's individuality has merged temporarily with that of the generic sinner whom Mary welcomes or whether he savours the tension between the sacred and the profane. Later in the chapter on the verge of his confession Stephen repeats the whole passage from Newman's address. As we shall see, by this point recitation has become an enactment of conformity. Initially, Stephen had been bewildered by sinfulness of uttering sacred names (presumably in a litany), whereas now he recites the lines as a prayer which apostrophises the Virgin Mary as a spiritual guide and refuge.

From an early stage in Chapter 3 Miltonic allusions alert us to the fact that Stephen is casting himself as Satan the proud sinful rebel. The recurring figure of the fall reinforces Stephen's haughty detachment from his fellow students but the sequence of this chapter actually realises the worst fear of Milton's Satan: 'To bow and sue for grace / With suppliant knee . . . / that were low indeed.'[3] That is exactly what Stephen does. His stance as would-be Satan falters before the impact of the sermons; he admits shame, mentally 'abasing himself'; and he finally kneels before his confession and at his concluding communion. Ironically, Stephen's spiritual rebirth is signalled through a new Miltonic and therefore Protestant analogy which recasts him as Adam being expelled from Paradise ('life lay all before him'). Significantly (see below, Chapter 4), the figure of Eve has been elided from the analogy, but in that respect Joyce was following the precedents of Dickens and George Eliot, who (in the concluding lines to Part I of *Great Expectations* and to Book II of *The Mill on the Floss* respectively) use this same allusion to signal the end of their protagonists' childhood. Stephen's symbolic gesture of submission coincides with an allegorisation of his mental conflicts into a battle between his guardian angel and a demon. This figure tacitly acknowledges his need of external help and paves the way to his confession. Later in the novel, when Stephen declares 'I will not serve', Cranly's rejoinder ('that remark was made before') reminds us of the complex and multiple nature of Stephen's repetitions. Not only is he recalling an earlier role which he could not sustain, but he is also repeating the preacher's quotation from Jeremiah during the retreat. The preacher makes the intertextual reference explicit by presenting Satan/Lucifer to the boys as an object lesson. So, paradoxically, Stephen is quoting from the very text whose authority he is questioning.

Joyce's use of Miltonic and biblical imagery in Chapter 3 is designed to highlight the drama taking place within Stephen's psyche over his sense of guilt. The following passage starts as a revery over his scribbler:

> The dull light fell more faintly upon the page whereon another equation began to unfold itself slowly and to spread abroad its widening tail. It was his own soul going forth to experience, unfolding itself sin by sin, spreading abroad the balefire of its burning stars and folding back upon itself, fading slowly, quenching its own lights and fires. They were quenched: and the cold darkness filled chaos. (*P*, 106)

The preceding analogy with a peacock's tail gives a traditional indication of pride and renders 'unfold' as a pun which predicts Stephen's separation from the true fold. 'Bale' is normally paired with its opposite 'bliss', a predictive reference to the state Stephen will reach by the end of the chapter. The 'burning stars' suggest both Lucifer and Wormwood, and help to orchestrate the imagery around polarities. So expansion immediately gives way to contraction, light to darkness. The penultimate sentence echoes Gloucester's description of a 'hell-black night' in *King Lear* when the sea 'quench'd the stelled fires' (III.vii.59–60).

Gloucester's words and the visionary narrative in Revelation both describe a disruption of the natural order which Stephen introjects into his own psyche. Inverting the biblical creation myth (and reinforcing it later in the chapter through a fantasy of flood), Joyce builds up an internal landscape of darkness and chaos as a composite image of Stephen's confusion, and by so doing demonstrates how far Stephen's imagination has been penetrated by Christian myth.

The ordering of information on Stephen's spiritual life gradually rises to a physical and moral climax in the nightmare he experiences after the sermons on Hell, and at every point Joyce underlines Stephen's assimilation of Catholic dogma and ritual. His physical position at the beginning of the chapter, sitting inside his classroom looking through the window at the world outside, metaphorically encapsulates his relation to the Church, a relation which the discourse elaborates. Even his reputation for asking awkward questions in the catechism class could be taken as a subversive extension of those very catechetical methods. Stephen presses his intellectual queries into those 'silences' where scholastic theology might lapse. Privately trying to apply the method of dialogue/catechism, Stephen only succeeds in assembling a list of unanswerable questions far more elaborate than those which embarrass his mother in *Stephen Hero*.

It is important for examples of this questioning to be given because it tilts the chapter initially towards an unorthodoxy which the sermons then correct; and it is equally important that Stephen's private questions have no answers since he has created a mental labyrinth for himself ('his mind wound itself in and out of the curious questions proposed to it'). The questions stand in an almost parasitic relation to the catechism, since without its simple and categorical explanations of doctrine Stephen's queries would have no meaning. He is attempting at least a partial independent ideological life from the Church in appropriating its didactic question-and-answer method to his own purposes, although even here an irony emerges. At the beginning Stephen's quasi-sacerdotal role is described as he leads his sodality through the little office of the Virgin Mary, and Kevin Sullivan has shown that the next chapter of *A Portrait* draws directly on the *Sodality Manual*.[4] By the end of the chapter, however, Stephen has regressed back to childhood in his conformity to the patterns of prayer and confession, as nostalgic as Henry Vaughan in 'The retreat' for his lost 'angel infancy'.

The retreat, of course, comprises the main narrative sequence of Chapter 3. So far we have been mainly concerned with preliminaries. We now need to look at how Joyce builds up the suspense. Primarily he uses a method of expansion where larger and larger homiletic blocks appear: firstly, the retreat is announced and dedicated to St Francis Xavier; secondly, the term 'retreat' is defined and an initial appeal made to the boys' attention to exclude worldly considerations: thirdly, the retreat proper finally gets under way with the 'death and judgement' section. Everything is arranged according to a set order, whether in ritual or in the logical coherence of the sermons which follow a pattern of biblical quotation, dedication and enumeration by breaking down the topic into component parts. Long after he had lost his faith Joyce maintained a respect for the Catholic Church as a masterpiece of institutional expositional system. Later in his life he told the sculptor August Suter that one of the benefits of his Jesuit upbringing was: 'I have learnt to arrange things in such a way that they become easy to survey and to judge' (E, 27). And later in *A Portrait* Stephen tells Cranly of his lingering admiration for an 'absurdity which is logical and coherent'.

In spite of its obvious importance the sermon on death and judgement is initially presented in indirect speech, perhaps to set up the immediacy of the two addresses on Hell, but a crucial aspect of voice emerges here. Bruce Bradley has suggested that the rector of Belvedere is not named because he is the 'representative of powers which threaten to swallow Stephen's individuality'.[5] In other words he personifies a function. But, even more importantly, his voice shades into that of the priest conducting the retreat, and the latter's blurs into the voices of the Bible. Consider the following passage on the deity:

> He speaks: and His voice is heard even at the farthest limits of space . . . . Supreme judge, from His sentence there will be and can be no appeal. He calls the just to His side . . . . The unjust he casts from Him, crying in his offended majesty: *Depart from me, ye cursed, into everlasting fire which was prepared for the devil and his angels. (P, 117)*

God's omnipotence is expressed as a voice which cannot be missed, a voice which reaches right across the universe. It is a commonplace for a preacher to quote from the Bible but it is also vital to realise that at these points the preacher is assuming a borrowed voice, temporarily magnifying his utterance beyond the limits of an individual speaker. This is what happens in all three sermons. The quotations from the saints and the Bible all converge on the ultimate voice, identified in the passage above as God's. The specific quotation from Matthew 25.xli is itself a quotation since Jesus is predicting the words of God on the day of judgement. Similarly, on the next page the preacher quotes Addison in turn quoting from I Corinthians 15 on his deathbed. And thanks to the labours of Joyce scholars we now know that the sermons on Hell consist largely of passages lifted from the tracts of Giovanni Pinamonti and Charles Gobinet, given minor modifications to intensify their negative impact.[6] In the first examples the act of quotation involves a submergence of the self of the speaker within his discourse and that is why the priest is referred to repeatedly as 'the preacher'. The exact identity of the speaker thus keeps shifting according to which particular allusions and quotations are in use. To maximise the dramatic impact of judgement the preacher shifts into direct speech and to maximise the power of God's voice pauses impressively after

'He speaks.' Utterance is all. The subsequent elaborations on speaking ('sentence', 'calls', 'crying', etc.) reinforce the evocation of God's majesty and also strengthen the themes of the novel since the next chapter will examine whether Stephen has a 'call' to the priesthood or not.

Just as the preacher becomes a disembodied voice so Stephen's ego is literally swallowed up by his discourse. When he imagines his death as a progressive smothering of the senses (including, significantly, his voice), it is impossible to pinpoint where summarised thought turns into summarised sermon because Stephen's imagined individual fate becomes a generic one. He becomes the sinner quaking before the seat of judgement. Accordingly, our sense of Stephen's consciousness gradually attenuates out of existence as past or predictive narrative ('every sin would then come forth') gives way to direct speech and an overwhelming emphasis on the present moment. Each interval between the sermons reveals Stephen's impressionability towards their language and imagery which he repeats in his thoughts. And the preamble to the chapter makes it clear that the sermons do not simply invade Stephen's consciousness. The discourse is already lodged there waiting to be brought out. The sermons simply make explicit the references to the fall and in the process totally assimilate Stephen's consciousness into their own discourse. It is accordingly through this rhetorical consequence that the sermons enact their authority. Temporarily the collective voice of the preacher erases all others in Stephen's consciousness and therefore suspends his separate identity as an individual.

The two main sermons constitute the climax of Chapter 3 and, although their power has regularly received a token nod from the critics (David Hayman, for instance, declared that the priest is a 'master of the affective'), there has been hardly any attempt to examine their rhetorical procedures.[7] Because they are given at length and because their discourse stands out from the general surrounding narrative (they are what Hayman rightly describes as insets) their rhetoric becomes foregrounded. Not only does the absence of mediation put us temporarily in the position of Stephen, but the stylization of the rhetoric enables us to see how the priest's listeners are being worked on. Although the sermons are about the power of God, in effect they demonstrate primarily the power of their own verbal persuasion. The speaker has the task of making Hell immediate to the boys and one tactic he uses towards this end is to evoke a worldly (and therefore familiar) image as a prelude to its intensification beyond the human dimension. This is related in turn to the device of the provisional superlative. The priest identifies an extreme again as a prelude to greater and greater intensification introduced by contrasters like 'and yet' or 'but'. The device can create self-parody, as when the priest invites the boys to imagine the smell of a single corpse (how many would be able to draw on their experience?) and then brings in a heavy battery of intensifiers so that Hell contains a stench 'multiplied a millionfold and a millionfold again from the millions upon millions of fetid carcasses massed together in the reeking darkness' (*P*, 124). The preacher establishes a dialogue between the boys' imagination and his own, between the things of this world and the region of the damned. He asks rhetorical questions; he pairs twinned qualities; he builds up to local climaxes through repeating the same phrasal pattern. Indeed, sometimes the repetition is so pronounced that it takes on an incantatory quality almost independent of meaning. The sound of a clock ticking introduces, for instance, an alternation between 'ever' and 'never' which expands in antithetical phrasing and as the phrases contract, returns to its basic opposition: 'ever, never; ever, never'. The antitheses of Chapter 1 are now marshalled into doctrinal order.

Such oppositions between the worldly and the spiritual collapse together in the paradoxes of Hell itself. Although it is described as a 'strait and dark and foul-smelling prison', it is also a place of infinite extent. Its qualities prove to be malleable since everything depends on the specific effect the

priest is aiming at – whether confinement or a minimalisation of human power. Similarly, the mode of address shifts
according to local purpose. At the beginning of the first
sermon the preacher invites a collaborative exercise of the
imagination ('let us try'), whereas the concluding climax
levels a barrage of direct accusatory questions at the boys
('why did you not shun the occasions of sin?' etc.). At this
point the priest is casting himself as the boys' conscience,
engaging in a kind of religious theatre to stimulate
acknowledgement of their guilt. When he declares 'God
spoke to you by so many, but you would not hear' he is in
effect commenting on the potential efficacy of his own
sermon.

The spiritual voices of Chapter 3 present us with a special
case of dialogics. Bakhtin's main examples in his study of
Dostoevsky and in his essay 'Discourse in the novel'
demonstrate how voices play against each other and reveal
themselves by difference. However a later essay, 'The
problem of the text' explicitly denies that opposition is the
only condition of dialogics which can, he insists, include
'pious acceptance'.[8] If so, then it would include the specific
rhetorical strategies pursued by Stephen's spiritual mentors
during the retreat, strategies which are designed to articulate
the collective authority of the Catholic Church. The identity
of the priest conducting that retreat is disclosed as Father
Arnall, a displaced presence from Stephen's past at
Clongowes, and then deindividualised as 'the preacher'. For
the most part Joyce even avoids this label and tag-phrases like
'he said', not only to render the sermons with immediacy but
also to signal to the reader that this is a voice which contains
other voices. The sermons embed quotations within quotations, from the Bible, the saints and even ludicrously from
an eye-witness who has supposedly seen the Devil. Utterance
now evokes community. As we shall see, the preacher voices
the cumulative tradition of the Church. His voice is an
expanding one which temporarily thrusts the boys to a
distance in order to maximise their realisation of sin and

which then concludes the second sermon with a series of questions drawing them rhetorically into the community of the repentant. Now the pronouns are collective: 'will we spit upon that face ...?' The punch-line of Mr Casey's Christmas-dinner story here becomes revised into an act of desecration and the earlier opposition with Dante disappears only to be replaced by a presumption of assent. Just as all the Church's speakers merge rhetorically into one voice so the preacher draws the boys to him by anticipating and discarding their objections.

The careful rhetorical patterning of these sermons invites a particular kind of assent because the discourse is claiming such a special status for itself. Bakhtin has given the following explanation, which bears immediately on this section of the novel:

> The authoritative word demands that we acknowledge it, that we make it our own; it binds us, quite independent of any power it might have to persuade us internally; we encounter it with its authority already fused to it. The authoritative word is located in a distanced zone, organically connected with a past that is felt to be hierarchically higher. It is, so to speak, the word of the fathers. Its authority was already acknowledged in the past. It is a prior discourse. It is therefore not a question of choosing it from among other possible discourses that are its equal. It is given (it sounds) in lofty spheres, not those of familiar contact. Its language is a special (as it were, hieratic) language. It can be profaned. It is akin to taboo, i.e. a name that must not be taken in vain. (*DI*, 342)

In every sense the discourse confronting Stephen is the 'word of the fathers' stretching back through a line of patrilinear authority from the priests to the founders of the order and the fathers of the Church, back to the primal Word. The patterning of the rhetoric (the use of exemplary biography, quotation, question and answer, enumeration and especially formulae like 'in the name of the Father ...') demonstrates its claim to be qualitatively superior to ordinary discourse; and indeed its general authority comes to a sharp focus in the moment of divine judgement. Now the 'sentence' in both its senses becomes an utterance which raises Stephen's sense of guilt to fever pitch.

Bakhtin argues that authoritative discourse demands acquiescence. There is little room left for the respondent other than assent, and accordingly the culmination of the preaching section is marked by a radical simplification of the syntax of Stephen's thoughts: 'God had called him. Yes? What? Yes? ... He had died. Yes' (*P*, 128). Stephen's acceptance of the Church's discourse is enacted as an internalisation of its propositions and a hysterical repetition ('like voices') of the term which has by now become surcharged with emotional and spiritual significance: 'Hell! Hell ...!'

The rhetorical principle of dialogue – utterance and response – becomes a spiritual principle in this section of the novel. The most important repeated term is 'call', exemplified in the chapter's opening pages through a profane manifestation and then developed in an intensively spiritual direction as the chapter progresses. Different faculties of Stephen's become dissociated from each other by being given separate voices (belly, heart, head, etc.), and Joyce draws on the literary genre of the dialogue between the soul and the body to weave unconventional variations on the pattern: 'His soul was fattening and congealing into a gross grease, ... while the body that was his stood, listless and dishonoured' (*P*, 115). In anticipation of Stephen's breakfast at the beginning of Chapter 5 the soul is given a startlingly physical substantiality, whereas the seat of vitality is now located in the body. Joyce uses dialogue to articulate a struggle going on within Stephen's faculties for supremacy, creating an internal vocalisation of his confusion. That is why he is addressed variously by his stomach, soul and a hypostatisation of his pride. The voice of Stephen's conscience is therefore not just a personal one because, as Voloshinov puts it, 'where did I get this "personal" point of view from, if not from the point of view of the people I was brought up by and educated with ...?'[9] Conscience, in other words, involves an articulation of the self as seen by external judges. Stephen's willingness to recognise the call of his conscience grows out of his internalisation of the Church's collective voice and as such reflects a temporary acquiescence to the Church's authority.

In between the two main sermons the language representing Stephen's thoughts becomes temporarily disjointed as he partially assimilates the rhetoric of prayer and only manages the first two words of a confession. The fluidity with which the boys recite their act of contrition enacts by contrast, and again through the call and response pattern, the boys' co-operation in a collective spiritual act. The confused voices which Stephen hears in between the sermons (are they inner or outer?) now give way to an orderly pattern where the personalities of the respondents merge together in a collective voice. This point implies a harmony which Stephen never actually achieves, as Joyce hints through an allusion at the opening of the recitation. Stephen prays 'with his heart' (and therefore perhaps not his mind?), 'his tongue cleaving to his palate'. Not only is there a distinction suggested here between utterance and silence, but the reference to Psalm 137 ('If I do not remember thee let my tongue cleave to the roof of my mouth') ironically implies spiritual neglect at the very climax of Stephen's supposed resurgence of belief. The ironies multiply. So in the chapel when Stephen is waiting for the confessional he beats his breast not in token of contrition so much as a physical attempt to suppress the murmuring voice of the flesh. The dualism between body and spirit which the sermons exploit manifests itself in Stephen as a disequilibrium between rival voices. Although he prays, this is implied to be an anachronistic return to the voice of his childhood. And although he internalises the imagery, vocabulary and even the syntax of the sermons, his inner debate reflects a conflict between rival impulses: 'How could he utter in words to the priest what he had done? Must, must' (*P*, 143).

In Chapter 1 of *A Portrait* Stephen's participation in

prayer follows the same rhetorical pattern as his participation in his lessons. Whether the subject is evening prayer
or Latin declensions, both have to be learnt by rote and both
have to be recited when given the appropriate cues. Caryl
Emerson has glossed the special characteristics of recitation
as follows:

> In reciting, the language of others is authoritative: it is
> distanced, taboo, and there can be no play with the framing
> context. One cannot even entertain the possibility of doubting
> it; so one cannot enter into a dialogue with it. To change a
> word in a recitation is to make a mistake. The power of this
> kind of language, however, has its corresponding cost: once
> discredited, it becomes a relic, a dead thing.[10]

Precisely because the words to be recited cannot be changed,
they stubbornly remain the discourse of others. However,
between Stephen's early schooldays and the retreat there
intervenes an episode – the Whitsun play – which renders
scholarly and spiritual authority as theatre and which
therefore alerts us to the possibility of covert disengagement
within the act of recitation. By forcing a disparity between
Stephen's feelings and the *Confiteor* Joyce prepares us for
the complex shifts of tone we have just been considering in
Chapter 3. It opens with Stephen in the position of a prayer
leader reciting prayers in a 'veiled voice' and closes with him
as respondent, but in both cases the text signals imbalances
between feeling and utterance, mind and body. The 'living
rail of hands' which includes Stephen within the line of boys
kneeling for communion is a precarious image because
Stephen has already withdrawn himself from the collectivity
of believers, but without recognising that withdrawal.

The confession appropriately rounds off this chapter
because it makes explicit the dialogue pattern which had
been established earlier through references to the catechism.
It comprises a question-and-answer sequence which tantalisingly replaces Stephen's most private admissions with figures
of physical voiding ('the last sins oozed forth'). In that
respect Joyce deliberately blocks off the most sensitive area

of Stephen's confession: namely, how to verbalise certain acts. It is more important that Stephen should participate at all in the verbal patterns of a sacrament which he will later refuse, and one irony of the scene lies in the fact that the confessor's repetition of 'my child' reminds the reader of a lost and irrecoverable innocence in Stephen more than the saving grace of forgiveness. Right to the very end of the chapter the references to dream as against waking life, to the body as against the mind, suggest that the dialectic between different parts of Stephen's psyche will continue. For all its spiritual appearance the confession turns out to have an ultimately secular significance. On the face of things, the confession signals an acceptance of a conformity to the forms of the Church comparable to the ending of Chapter 1.

A further irony of the sermons emerges when we remember that Stephen's ambitions to become an artist necessitate breaking away from the Catholic Church. His developing sense of literature involves symbolic coherence, intellectual clarity, narrative skill and a capacity to digest the lessons of earlier writers. All these qualities are demonstrated in the retreat addresses. The references to apocalypse and the Virgin Mary are made through systematic imagery and symbolism which Stephen explicitly recognises in the Catholic liturgy. The preacher rehearses the primal narrative of Christian culture: namely, the fall of man. He again uses a well-tried method in inviting the boys to create a picture of Hell ('imagine . . . imagine' runs like a refrain through his words), and, as we have seen, expounds his subject by breaking it down into component parts. Quotations from the Bible, earlier literature and figures like St Thomas (who becomes Stephen's mentor in the final chapter) not only bolster the authority of his words but also demonstrate his capacity to assimilate. And so the very institution which Stephen purports to be rebelling against will turn out to have realised or at least shaped his literary ideals.

Stephen's apparent acquiescence to the Church continues into the next chapter whose opening section shows how he has mapped out his life in an effort to stem the 'flood of temptation'. Once again the principle of division and enumeration is followed, so that separate days have their own dedication and separate senses receive their own mortification. The external collective activity of the college slides easily into the personal internal activity of Stephen himself because he has accepted so unreservedly the methods proposed by Catholic books of devotion, the popularity of which at this time for Cheryl Herr marks the 'extreme codification of Catholic theology'.[11] The stylistic method of this section is a kind of extended quotation as if the devotional instructions have been recast in indirect speech. Only one author is named – St Alphonsus Liguori, who in 1723 had the mystical experience of hearing an inner voice call him to withdraw from the world and join the priesthood, which he did the following year. For the moment we leave Stephen's 'inner voice' to contemplate the elaborate defensive scheme he has created to ward off the temptations of this world. Bakhtin has identified what he calls a 'hidden polemic' in the reproduction of another's discourse within the author's because the one acts upon the other 'while remaining outside it'.[12] To a certain extent this is what happens in the summary of Stephen's devotional exercises. Joyce uses three devices to disrupt the flow of this summary: verbal echoes from *Marius the Epicurean*, an analogy which hints at the materialistic nature of his spiritual calculations and an echo of the description which closes Chapter 2. The first hints at fantasy in Stephen as if 'he was kneeling at mass in the catacombs'. The second disrupts the area of spiritual reference by injecting an obtrusively worldly note: his soul seems to be operating a 'great cash register'. The third example simply transposes an erotic image (a swooning kiss) into a new context while retaining the same physical vocabulary.

As usual in *A Portrait*, the summary of Stephen's devotional texts reminds us that this is a mediated account and leaves a rhetorical gap between the discourse and the activities of the protagonist. The more the discourse is disrupted, the more this gap widens. Ignatius Loyola's *Spiritual Exercises* state that exterior penance should be the 'fruit' of interior penance, but this notional harmony between inner and outer becomes more and more problematic in the novel. The textual ironies, reinforced by Joyce's emphasis on the materiality of Alphonsus Liguori's book ('with fading characters and sere foxpapered leaves'), create a psychic space which Stephen himself attempts to fill by addressing rebellious areas of his self. This local section concludes significantly with an unanswered question ('I have amended my life, have I not?') which takes on greater implications in view of what happens next.

The coda to Chapter 3 properly occurs in the succeeding one, when Stephen is invited to consider whether he has a vocation to the priesthood. This scene demonstrates the last time the Church will exert solicitations on Stephen but, of course, does not end its impact on his imagination. It is also the scene which examines the most solemn meaning of 'call'. The summons to the director's office is a prelude to an altogether more weighty invitation just as his small-talk is a preamble to the main subject. Kevin Sullivan has argued that there is a double perspective in this episode: 'the priest is preoccupied with thoughts of sin and the redeeming effect of grace; the artist is busy portraying the sinner and parodying the ways of grace. For parody is his mode, as prayer is the mode proper to the priest.'[13] The perspective from Stephen is not quite parodic, however. Rather, the scene demonstrates an ironic sequence of call and response which fits neither the requirements of spiritual vocation nor those of ordinary dialogue. At the beginning of the section we are made aware of the priest's tone of voice rather than his appearance or his words. Once again an unnamed official of the Church exerts a primarily vocal presence, but this time Stephen is conscious of being worked on and, as it were, stands off from the situation in silence. However, when the priest broaches the question of the priesthood Stephen's reaction is almost instinctive: ' "Have you ever felt that you had a vocation?" Stephen parted his lips to answer yes and then withheld the word suddenly' (*P*, 160). His outer response is blocked off – he never actually replies to the priest here – but inwardly the director's appeal to the seductions of power (a term repeatedly stressed by him) triggers off an immediate reaction in Stephen's mind, where he silently rehearses the ordination service. The outer voice finds an echoing inner voice forcing itself on Stephen's consciousness: 'through the words he heard even more distinctly a voice bidding him approach, offering him secret knowledge and secret power'. The scene's alternation between inner and outer is here given vocal expression as what amounts to a temptation.

In August 1904 Joyce wrote to Nora: 'six years ago I left the Catholic Church, hating it most fervently . . . . Now I make open war upon it by what I write and say and do' (*E*, 169). We have seen this hostility implicit in the ironies of Chapter 3, where the Church's collective voice temporarily erases Stephen's identity. After the 'vocation' episode a number of different means are used to set Stephen at a distance from the Church. Firstly, the collective voice of the institution is replaced by the individual voices of its members, who pose far less of an intellectual threat to Stephen. Secondly, Stephen appropriates the doctrine of the Church (transubstantiation, God as creator, etc.) to his own secular aesthetic purposes just as Joyce himself uses the seasons of the Catholic year to structure *A Portrait*. And thirdly, he reduces Catholic ritual to a series of games or performances. In Chapter 2 we see the first example of this comic distancing when Stephen recites the *Confiteor* to his school-fellows but is curiously drawn to an enigmatic young Jesuit who could represent a potential self to him at that point. This refusal of reverence is picked up again in Dylan Thomas's *Portrait of the Artist as a Young Dog* (1940), when the boy Gwilym transforms a local barn into a substitute Protestant chapel complete with lighting (a candle) and pulpit (a cart). He attempts to lead the boys in confessions but the game turns serious when the narrator/protagonist remembers his sins but refuses to perform his role. When he declares 'I haven't done anything bad' he is admitting, not innocence, but an inability to distance himself from the oppressive influence of the chapel.[14]

Throughout Chapter 5 of *A Portrait* references to the Church are either negative or disengage respect from religious belief. C. G. Anderson has demonstrated that the opening of the chapter travesties the celebration of the mass and ensuing ritual for Maundy Thursday with Stephen performing centrally as mock-priest. A brief and apparently passing comparison identifies the analogy between Stephen, Temple and Cranly, and a 'celebrant attended by his ministers on his way to the altar'. Anderson shows that Stephen traverses an area, performs acts and makes statements which resemble Catholic ritual and which thus put his expositions of theory in an ironic context since he is performing his 'symbolic office as Stephen–Christ, the first priest of art'.[15] The apparently naturalistic surface of text invites a superficial reading of Stephen's comments on the Maundy Thursday hymns as an aesthetic appreciation of a religious work, but Anderson supplies the data for recognising the whole chapter as a kind of palimpsest, written over the Catholic ritual, which casts his sister in the role of acolyte and his mother as server. This sort of superscription reduces the Catholic ritual or biblical narratives (like the divine conception, or crucifixion) to depressed analogies, and presents Joyce's narrative as an anti-text enacting its opposition to the Church through travesty.

Joyce went on to develop this method in *Ulysses*, which opens with a comic imitation of the mass, comic because it was wrenched out of context and applied to the more mundane ritual of shaving. A new character officiates, however. Buck Mulligan rivals Stephen's cherished role as irreverent mocker through his ability to improvise profane variations on the words of the service. At the beginning of the Circe episode

Stephen tries to regain primacy of utterance by reciting the paschal introit to Lynch, but this only succeeds as a repetition of the last scenes of *A Portrait* and demonstrates no verbal virtuosity. The Catholic mass is constantly present in *Ulysses* whether as a text to gloss, as a service to witness or as a ritual to invert; and that presence represents one aspect of the ubiquitous influence of the Church on Joyce's writing.

3

Stephen as Artist: The Context of the Villanelle

Stephen's attitude to the Catholic Church involves both rejection and assimilation. It would be grossly simplistic to view the Church, therefore, as only an obstacle to artistic expression. The draft essay 'A portrait of the artist' has its protagonist declare 'I have left the Church', but he immediately plunges into the 'hierarchs of initiation' (figures such as St John of the Cross) and emerges with a persistently spiritual purpose formed: namely, 'to reunite the children of the spirit'.[1] Similarly, *Stephen Hero* questions – much more explicitly than *A Portrait* – Stephen's desire to detach his imagination from all trace of Catholicism through a critical anonymous voice: 'was it anything but vanity which urged him to seek out the thorny crown of the heretic while the entire theory, in accordance with which his entire artistic life was shaped, arose most conveniently for his purpose out of the mass of Catholic theology?' (*SH*, 209). These 'nimble pleaders' are left unnamed, as if they are articulating a sceptical side to Stephen's own consciousness, and both works imply that his development as an artist is a complex product of his experience as a Catholic. We now need to trace out the growth of this artistic purpose. At Clongowes we saw that Stephen begins to draw elementary distinctions between words, usages and sounds. An important part of this process involves poetry and song. Unlike the autobiographies of Yeats and Moore, or such narratives of growing sensibility as *Marius the Epicurean* and Huysmans' A

Rebours, Joyce does not privilege the influence on his protagonist of one particular book or writer, but instead shows that literature is a constant presence from Stephen's earliest childhood onwards. Poetry has to be identified like anything else in Chapter 1 by distinguishing between its opposite, so that Stephen reads lines backwards as an experiment and even asks himself if formally arranged lists have literary value. Three things happen in this chapter which have a crucial bearing on Stephen's subsequent desire to become an artist: firstly, the nexus of associations between beauty and loss or death is established; then, since repetition acts as a heuristic tool to discovering meaning, Stephen applies this practice to poetry and begins his interest in the sound-values of words and rhyme; lastly, a dialectic is set up between high poetry and the ribald rhymes of Stephen's school-fellows which extends right into the last chapter of the novel. There the languor of his villanelle contrasts variously with the vigour of Renaissance songs, the grandeur of processional hymns and the bawdy energy of the students' rhymes. From the very beginning of the novel Joyce contextualises poetical forms so that they rebound off each other and collectively suggest the ranges of expression available to Stephen at that historical moment.

Stephen's poetic programme in *Stephen Hero* is summarised concisely: 'He sought in his verses to fix the most elusive of his moods', a plan which derives from Arthur Symons via Yeats (*SH*, 37). The former exclaimed in his preface to *London Nights* (1897): 'The moods of men! There I find my subject', and Joyce himself followed Yeats in entitling an early collection of his verse *Moods* (E, 50). *Stephen Hero*, however, does not show this creed in practice. Rather, Stephen engages in a private polemic against a bourgeois notion of artistic production, asserting instead the Flaubertian principle of style being the end result of artistic labour. In the earlier novel priority is given to Stephen's aesthetic formulations at the expense of any actual poetic creativity he might show, and Joyce stresses his eagerness to participate in the ferment of critical debate taking place in what he sardonically refers to as the 'city of the arts'.

One axiom which Stephen expounds to Cranly is particularly useful to understanding the creative process in *A Portrait*: 'To apprehend it [the beautiful object] you must lift it away from everything else' (*SH*, 217). This principle of abstraction operates the first time that we witness Stephen trying to compose poetry. The third section of Chapter 2 demonstrates his uneasy attempts to follow literary and ecclesiastical authority; Byron supplies the precedent for his title but Jesuit practice supplies the opening and concluding initials: AMDG (*ad majorem dei gloriam*) and LDS (*laus deo semper*). The method of composing a theme ironically structures his artistic composition. Not only that: while he is waiting for inspiration Stephen remembers trying to write a poem on the back of one of his father's legal notices. Here in miniature we find rendered concretely the distinction between verbal value which Stephen articulates in Chapter 5 as a contrast between art and the market place. His poetry can only come into being through a struggle with learnt formulae of expression and the prosaic details of the experience which might trigger that poetry. Although Stephen appeals to his memory, artistic expression actually involves the erasure of many remembered details. So, when Stephen is looking back at the failed romantic episode he wants to express (the passage – originally an epiphany – which begins 'It was the last tram') he first of all filters out the circumstances which would actualise the situation, blurs the male and female figures within it and reduces the verbal range of the poem: 'The verses told only of the night and the *balmy breeze* and the *maiden lustre of the moon*' (*P*, 72; my italics). The italicised phrases appear within implied quotation marks as befits clichés of romantic lyricism and Joyce implies here, as elsewhere in the novel, that Stephen's attempts at originality boil down to a recycling of learnt phraseology. The narrative summarises Stephen's poetic attempt in a tone whose very neutrality mocks the attempt. Because the narrative voice at this point is clearly not Stephen's it suggests the destructive effects scrutiny by a third party could have. Stephen hides his book specifically to exclude the possibility of another breaking the charmed circle of romantic wish-fulfilment. Similarly, he anticipates the ridicule his villanelle would provoke at Emma's house, excluding a readership even before the poem has been composed.

The tension in the first episode between poetic exaltation and the mundane realities of life is repeated in Dylan Thomas's *Portrait of the Artist as a Young Dog*, where the narrator recites passages from his poems while the sounds of his home town force themselves on his consciousness. Thomas does not show the actual composition of the poems and so the prose does not feed the poetry as it does in the villanelle section of *A Portrait*. Instead, the poems of Thomas's narrator stand in ironic opposition to the 'respectable autumn evening' of their recital. They exert a private gesture of protest against the decencies of the boy's social context by covertly admitting to illicit appetites, to the 'thoughts that issue' from the mind's 'well of furtive lust'.[2]

Stephen's famous epiphany at the end of Chapter 4 can also be read as a poetic composition, although Joyce never states that he actually puts pen to paper. This time Stephen physically enacts the process of abstraction by positioning himself apart from the other boys who are swimming, recoiling from the 'corpselike' pallor of their bodies, which remind him of his own mortality. The crucial difference between this episode and the passage just discussed is that the rhythm of Stephen's thoughts is now given in considerable detail. As we would expect, his mounting excitement is articulated as the response to a voice and as silent exclamations. The summons to the priesthood has become transformed into the 'call of life', and the whole episode dramatises Stephen's rejection of the former by a reapplication of religious terms to his own aesthetic and physical development. He conflates spiritual rescue ('deliverance'),

Advent and the imagery of the Easter resurrection in a daring reversal of priorities, where the religion of his boyhood becomes part of the 'cerements shaken from the body of death'. Notionally, Stephen's perceived surge of vitality can only be explained in opposition to the spiritual system against which he is rebelling. However, when the girl standing in midstream is described, Hugh Kenner argues persuasively that the effect is not of unmediated excitement or just an overblown style, but rather like a 'young man's copybook page: . . . something like a piece he might have written out afterwards, practising his new vocation.' Kenner continues with a detailed commentary on the key paragraph:

> We should reflect that Stephen would have been 16, and would be working from the kind of preliminary outline in which his Jesuit masters had drilled him. So a topic sentence proposes the optical fact, a girl, and a second sentence rolls up its sleeves to state what the paragraph will elucidate, that she seems changed by magic into the likeness of a seabird. Four more sentences deal with this statement as though it were a proposition to be demonstrated; each, beginning with 'Her', affirms something birdlike of a separate part of her body, the scan proceeding upward, her legs, her thighs, her waist, her bosom. Then an orderly 'But', when we come to hair and face, affirms the unvanquished categories of girlishness, with the solemnly cadenced chiasmus to achieve finality.[3]

Kenner demonstrates that at the very point of celebrating his supposed liberation from the Church Stephen structures the moment of lyrical intensity according to the expository methods of the Jesuits.

Joyce has temporarily objectified Stephen's discourse and there results an uncertainty over time and perspective because, as Bakhtin puts it, 'such discourse is not only double-voiced but also double-accented.'[4] Briefly, it becomes impossible to distinguish Stephen's words from the narrator's and the only way in which we can deconstruct the episode to locate its internal contradictions is to perform the close syntactic analysis Kenner recommends, or to scrutinise the verbal details to note, for instance, his excited list of purposes ('to live, to err, to fall, to triumph, to recreate life out of life!') which suggests in miniature a sequence of sin, lapse and resurgence. The internal climax of Stephen's excitement, a swoon of ecstasy, is expressed in an image echoing Dante. Here the intertextual ironies begin to multiply. Just as Stephen sees a girl standing in midstream, rhapsodises on her beauty and then finds that she has disappeared; so at the end of *Paradise* Dante witnesses Beatrice standing in a river of light, is distracted and in Canto 31 turns to discover that she too has vanished. Stephen's ecstasy is phrased as 'a breaking light, an opening flower'; Dante's culminating vision is of the celestial rose, perpetually opening in an endless spring. This rose, however, represents divine love in containing within itself the souls of the redeemed, whereas Stephen's flower transposes religious ecstasy on to the profane colour of crimson and disperses his feelings on to a secularised scene. Where Dante glimpses a collectivity, Stephen's experience has the contour of a mystical visitation ('a wild angel had appeared to him') which heightens his *individual* self-consciousness (G, 146). And the repeated stress on individual novelty (the experience initiates Stephen into 'some new world') is counteracted by the passage's verbal and imagistic dependence on earlier texts like Yeats's poem 'The wanderings of Oisin', which supplies many of the descriptive details of the scene. In Yeats the seashore is the place of departure from which Oisin and Niamh embark on a transcendental journey through the air and into the ocean's depths. Stephen's flight of the imagination is more short-lived, but is articulated as a response ('her eyes had called to him and his soul had leaped at the call') and a passage through thresholds, through the 'gates of all the ways of error and glory'. We are now in a position to see how the same interplay between invention and derivation occurs during the composition of Stephen's villanelle. Here again we shall see the process of abstraction at work, this time with more complex results.

The whole account of how Stephen composes his poem is

shot through with ironies surrounding its derivation. The Bakhtinian principle that 'an utterance is never *in itself* originatory' finds confirmation in the particular irony Joyce applies to Stephen's attempts at composition, for he insistently places the latter within a context of social or cultural circumstances.[5] Indeed, it is impossible for Joyce to introduce a villanelle into *A Portrait* without the reader speculating on its links with the main practitioner of that form in the 1890s – Ernest Dowson. Influenced, like Joyce, by Verlaine's subtle sound-effects, Dowson uses the villanelle partly as a means of reducing his range of poetic expression. It is a verse form unusually dependent on repetition (only two rhymes, within which the first and third lines of the opening tercet must recur). Linda Dowling has argued that this suited Dowson because 'his reduction of poetic symbols to a very few confers upon them the power of abstract variables whose meaning resides in a system – a system, moreover, that is largely indifferent to the usual responsibilities of representation.'[6] In a similar way Stephen's villanelle weaves three variations on the figure of rising with its connotations of worship and its lexical reversal of 'fallen' in the second line. The poem plays on the etymological sense of 'ardent' (burning) through association by rhyme ('ardent ways'/'ablaze') to concentrate attention on the relation of the poem's addressee to the speaking male voice. Although the former is a 'lure' and therefore the poem is articulating an enervated complaint, the images of verses 3 and 4 suggest tribute and even thanksgiving ('eucharistic'). Dowling locates in Dowson a wearied sense of endings which again features prominently in the villanelle. The sexual fever suggested in the second verse has receded into the past as a series of repeated acts, whereas the present attenuates the poem's utterance into '*broken* cries' and draws out the penultimate moment ('tell no more') of fascination into an extended present through long open vowels and alliteration. The poem appears to circle around its own languor through its repetitions, requesting an answer but also yearning for silence. Because the subject of the phrase 'tell no more' is omitted, it is as if the speaker were addressing himself, using the poem to express a desire for the poem to cease.

The account of Stephen's composition draws heavily on a Symbolist aesthetic. Joyce read *The Symbolist Movement in Literature* in 1900 with sufficient interest for phrases from it to recur in his own essays. He met Symons himself two years later and on the strength of that personal contact the latter was instrumental in getting *Chamber Music* published. A number of emphases in *The Symbolist Movement* shed light on the description of Stephen's composition. It is firstly born out of dream, as are the poems of Nerval and Rimbaud. It is brought into being by an attempt to arrest a passing ecstasy, which Symons identifies as a common purpose in Mallarmé's poetry. Unusually, he even tries to give a summary of the compositional process itself:

> He has received then, a mental sensation: let it be the horror of the forest. This sensation begins to form in his brain, at first probably no more than a rhythm, absolutely without words. Gradually thought begins to concentrate itself (but with an extreme care, lest it should break the tension on which all depends) upon the sensation, already struggling to find its own consciousness. Delicately, stealthily, with infinitely timid precaution, words present themselves, at first in silence. Every word seems like a desecration, seems, the clearer it is, to throw back the original sensation farther and farther into the darkness. But, guided always by the rhythm, which is the executive soul (as, in Aristotle's definition, the soul is the form of the body), words come slowly, one by one, shaping the message.[7]

Symons unconsciously identifies a paradox which recurs in Stephen's own experience: the closer the poet moves to verbal expression, the more he becomes aware of loss, the absence of what is being articulated. Where Symons presents verbalisation as an inevitable act of sacrilege, forcing the original sensation back into a pre-verbal void ('the darkness'), Stephen's inner struggles are directed towards recovering what might be lost, what might already be receding into the past ('the night *had been* enchanted . . . he *had known* the ecstasy').

The imaginative resources Stephen marshals to prevent this recession focus on the malleability of language; and here we should remember that on the opening page of *The Symbolist Movement* Symons notes the arbitrary significance of words. We shall see shortly how the linguistic diversity of Stephen's environment forces a similar consciousness on him. For Symons the Symbolists had incorporated this awareness into their exploitation of dream and fantasy where new possibilities of meaning are opened up. One of the main practitioners of this openness was Verlaine (whose poems Joyce started to translate in 1900). Words, we are told, become plastic in his hands: 'They transform themselves for him into music, colour, and shadow; a disembodied music, diaphanous colours, luminous shadow.'[8] Joyce's language too crosses into the non-verbal, evoking light as liquid and a spirit 'pure as the purest water, sweet as dew, moving as music'. The description of composing the poem goes through a series of imagistic transformations which centre on a cluster of words given the following iambic introduction: 'the rose-like glow sent forth its rays of rhyme'. The cluster raise/rose/ray conflates reverence, radiance and transition, and focuses a series of phrasal permutations, as we shall see in a moment. For Symons the Symbolist Movement represents a 'revolt against exteriority', a revolt which Stephen enacts by turning towards his bedroom wall in an effort to recapture his dream. The movement involves a poetic discipline which becomes itself a 'kind of religion' and it is correspondingly during this composition that Stephen privately casts himself as a 'priest of the eternal imagination'.

Before we see how Joyce bends the exalted aims of Symbolism towards irony we should recognise a second presence in this section of the novel, namely that of W. B. Yeats. His 1900 essay 'The symbolism of poetry' (which derives directly from Symons's study, of which Yeats was the dedicatee) describes a state so near to Stephen's that it seems as if this section of *A Portrait* was written to illustrate it:

> The purpose of rhythm, it has always seemed to me, is to prolong the moment of contemplation, the moment when we are both asleep and awake, which is the one moment of creation, by hushing us with an alluring monotony, while it holds us waking by variety, to keep us in that state of perhaps real trance, in which the mind liberated from the pressure of the will is unfolded in symbols.[9]

Obviously, Stephen is in the half-waking state outlined here, but Yeats's description is useful for identifying a cross-purpose in Stephen's composition. On the one hand, he is attempting to recover a recent experience; on the other, he is actually retarding that process, trying to draw out a state prior to full consciousness. Yeats suggests a Keatsian arrest, a suspension of transitions, which in Joyce's prose finds its expression in appositional phrases which slow down the movement of the syntax. The 'internal' passages are thus quite distinct rhetorically from those paragraphs giving external description. Throughout his essay Yeats stresses the resonances and suggestions of lines as does Stephen, and he even quotes the same line from Nash which later passes through Stephen's thoughts. Yeats notes the associations between the sounds of words, and both music and colour; and he privileges the function of the adjective which Joyce had parodied in the following lines by Stephen from *Stephen Hero*: 'The dawn awakes with tremulous alarms, / How grey, how cold, how bare!' (*SH*, 42). And Yeats cites the moon as a particularly potent symbol; Stephen correspondingly remembers Shelley's fragment 'To the moon' as a poetic evocation of human helplessness.

Joyce's narrative presents Stephen's 'creation' as deriving from such writers as Yeats and Symons; and shows artistic composition as a gradual emergence from a mental ground. The poem, accordingly, must be considered in relation to that ground, in relation to the fits and starts of what Stephen would call his 'inspiration'. The prose uses a variety of devices here to inch gradually forwards towards expression. Continuous verb-tenses draw out duration; repetition both examines and modulates the imagery; and paradoxically the time-indicators foreground the fact that the pivotal experience has passed even when they are evoking Stephen's state most immediately. Symons had taken Carlyle's definition of a symbol from *Sartor Resartus* ('some embodiment and revelation of the Infinite') in order to re-emphasise the access it granted to a transcendental dimension of meaning. That is why he is unusually hospitable to states of trance or dream, and why Yeats links rhythm with hypnosis as one means of expressing 'something that moves beyond the senses'.[10] Joyce, however, carefully sets up an ambiguity of reference so that the prose seems to oscillate between the physical and the spiritual. Stephen, as it were, awakes in layers to a 'morning inspiration' which is immediately re-expressed in physical terms ('inbreathed'). Little by little a series of religious analogies take shape whereby awakening becomes equated with creation and then impregnation.

At this point the first verse of the poem finds utterance, and here we need to consider the organisation of its imagery. Indeed, the whole poem could be read as a clever pastiche of the *fin-de-siècle* lyric. Robert Scholes, one of the few critics to look at the poem in any detail, has found parallels established between Eve and Mary, Gabriel and Satan. He continues: 'in the Bible Eve figures as first temptress as well as mother. And this feminine principle – irrational, sensual, seductive – becomes in Joyce's inversion of traditional typology equally the property of Mary and Eve.'[11] Scholes usefully identifies the ways in which Joyce bends Christian tradition to his own purposes, although a more likely figure than Eve would be Lilith, Adam's apocryphal first wife, who is presented by Dante Rossetti as a fatal enchantress, in other words as a sexual predator. The poem expresses a state of frustrated weariness that is itself a cliché from the 1890s, which implies a passive susceptibility of the collective male figures entirely consistent with Stephen's surrounding revery. The female addressee of the poem is never identified beyond her sexual attributes (the proud possessor of 'lavish limb') and in that respect comes to resemble the remote maiden depicted by Joyce's compatriot, James Clarence Mangan. In his 1907 lecture on that poet Joyce noted the same combination of desire and doom which informs his own poem:

> The figure which he adores recalls the spiritual yearnings and the imaginary loves of the Middle Ages, and Mangan has placed his lady in a world full of melody, lights and perfumes, a world that grows fatally to frame every face that the eyes of a poet have gazed on with love. (CW, 182–3)

The derivative nature of the poem's imagery and of its preliminary description undercuts Stephen's intensity by questioning its novelty, setting up echoes of Tennyson, Gray and other poets. Stephen's excitement is all directed inwards towards cherishing a private state of arousal, but one of the main points to this section of *A Portrait* is that Joyce forces a broader awareness on the reader by dramatising a conflict between Stephen's flagging imagination and the 'common noises' of life. A tension is established between the details of the poem and the circumstances of its composition. Once Stephen has reached the third verse the rhythm sustaining his composition peters out and his physical surroundings impinge on his imagination as day dawns. The perspective moves outside his consciousness to record his movements in a neutral, accurate and much more transitive prose, bathetically contrasting the image of him writing his verses on a cigarette packet with the introverted exaltation of his poem. Without needing to spell it out, Joyce exploits the reader's awareness of the novel to contrast two notions of art here. Stephen's is exclusive and only achieved by making a 'cowl' of his blanket, symbolically blocking out as much of the world as possible; whereas the novel's shows a dialectical interchange between Stephen's imagination and his day-to-day life. Stephen's memory takes him back to an

Irish class where the unnamed girl filling his thoughts is talking to a priest. In his imagination he rejects this rival image, just as in memory he had marched out of the room. Stephen's efforts here are directed towards filtering out memories which obstruct his drift in revery towards a singular self-image and a female *alter ego* who can 'yield' to him in the orgasmic moment when the whole poem can be uttered. Yeats too had evoked the creative meeting of mind and emotion in sexual terms, 'as a woman gives herself to a lover'.[12] This female figure is composed by Stephen out of a set of assumptions about sexuality, specifically out of the crude binary opposition between innocence and sin. He identifies the onset of her menstruation with his own sexual beginnings, conveniently finding in her a responsiveness to his own consciousness. The recitation of the full villanelle is then ushered in by the sexual swoon with which Stephen yields to this figure and the section of the novel symmetrically closes itself off with a return to the liquid matrix of imagery and even language itself: 'like a cloud of vapour or like waters circumfluent in space the liquid letters of speech, symbols of the element of mystery, flowed forth over his brain' (*P*, 227).

By spatialising Stephen's psyche Joyce reminds us of the abstracted and introverted nature of the aspiring poet's creation. This rhapsodic merging of the self with its own feminine *alter ego* actually dates Stephen's imaginings and places them within the context of 1980s double images. Jan B. Gordon explains the phenomenon as follows:

> The 'mirror-effect', so common in the life and art of the late nineteenth century, is thus a visual representation which unifies a number of divergent strains in the phenomenology of the nineties: the Doppelganger and the divided self; the voyeurism implicit in romantic self-consciousness; the highly polished surfaces of much Art Nouveau; the labyrinthine structure shared both by geographic quests and a language which seeks an ever more refined nuance. Yeats's statement

'no mind can engender till divided into two' – suggests that Narcissus must engage in perpetual warfare with some anti-self in order to prevent immersion in the pool of abstration.[13]

Although the female figure (waking like Stephen himself) is explicitly identified with the 'temptress of the villanelle', in the poem she functions as a more distinguishable other, rhetorically distinct from the speaker who addresses her. While her threatening aspect never takes on the force of Lionel Johnson's dark angel, for instance, she is more distanced than Stephen's erotic figure who 'enfolds him'.

Not only does Joyce set up intertextual ironies between the villanelle and the writings of his contemporaries, but even his own *Chamber Music* provides us with another point of access to the villanelle, because here we see him trying his hand at a sustained series of love lyrics. He originally planned the sequence as a two-part suite which was reordered by Stanislaus shortly before publication, and Robert Boyle has now demonstrated through a detailed commentary how the poems comprise a narrative which starts from yearning, pivots on a point of union and then concludes with reflections on the transience of love.[14] What is important to note in these poems is Joyce's use of different rhetorical devices of address. Initially, the speaker finds relief from his isolation by creating a dialogue between the night wind and ethereal harps playing to love, and Joyce thereby introduces a series of variations on the basic relation between singer and listener. This can be reversed and the speaker can briefly separate himself into witness and protagonist, but the urgency of the first part mounts as the speaker progressively tries to move towards union with his beloved. The climax approaches in poem 16 (xl in the published order) when the speaker bids the maiden to remove the symbolic vestments of maidenhood (zone and snood). Then it approaches still nearer in poem 17 which draws extensively on the Song of Songs to celebrate the imminent meeting of the lovers. Here the symbolism of the Virgin Mary blends in with the erotic imagery with no strain because Joyce has stylised the situation so successfully. Nothing disrupts the internal harmony of place with feeling or the alternations between address ('my dove, my beautiful one') and hortatory refrain ('arise, arise!'). Repetition plays as central a role in this lyric as it does in the villanelle. Our sense of the woman's presence in these poems also emerges from her having a voice (she also sings at one point), from her reaction to the 'lying clamour' of other voices trying to impose a consciousness of love as sin, and from the implied wealth of physical imagery lying behind the allusions to the Song of Songs. But there is an irony in these allusions. In *Stephen Hero* Stephen considers collecting his poems into a 'perfect wreath' modelled on Dante's *Vita Nuova*. This work celebrates the power of earthly love as an anticipation of spiritual bliss through a lexical overlap between 'Beatrice' and 'beatitude', but no such optimism is available to Joyce. *Chamber Music* hardly evokes a point of union before it recedes into a sombre recognition of separation and loss. Poem 19 (xv) repeats the call to the loved one to arise, this time to a consciousness of morning and therefore of impending departure.

The description of Stephen's villanelle reconstructs the two key lyrics in *Chamber Music* (17/xiv and 19/xv) by retaining the same dawn ingredients (fragrance, bells, etc.) while questioning them. Now the dawn does not imply the parting of the lovers so much as the near loss of the poem from Stephen's memory. Whereas the *Vita Nuova* systematically allows poems to grow out of inspirational dreams and then glosses their structure and significance, no such transcendental certainty is available to Stephen and by the end of *A Portrait* he has explicitly turned his back on the 'spiritual–heroic refrigerating apparatus, invented and patented in all countries by Dante Alighieri' (*P*, 256). *Chamber Music* stresses the fleeting relative nature of love; *A Portrait* questions the compositional experience itself ('was it an instant of enchantment only . . .?'). The process is encodedreligiously. Just as the girl standing on the shore at

the end of Chapter 4 is described as an image metamor-
phosed into a dove and therefore to be revered, so now
inspiration is expressed as an annunciation. Where earlier
the Virgin Mary either had been addressed directly or had
stood behind the other idealised images of feminity, now
Stephen actually *becomes* her as if the artist is trying to take
on the powers of motherhood. The flow of waters which
precedes the full text of the villanelle could now be read as
the moment of birth when Stephen produces not only his
artistic creation but also the Christ role which he cherishes
elsewhere in the last chapter. The biblical analogy with
creation implies that Stephen identifies more closely with the
Virgin after he has lost his faith and also sets up an
extraordinary oscillation between literal and analogical
gender throughout the passage. Stephen dramatises himself
not only as a phallic force and a female matrix (in his essay
on Mangan Joyce notes that the poet calls the imagination
the 'mother of things': CW, 182), but even as the foetus
which this self-engendering produces, thereby actualising the
word he saw carved in the Cork lecture theatre.

The more the outside world forces itself on Stephen's
consciousness the more the 'exquisite' order he theorises in
Stephen Hero becomes compromised. His cherished female
image fractures into the 'distorted reflections' of a flower-
girl, a kitchen-girl and others. While Stephen tries to sustain
what was described above as a 'mirror-effect' by exclusion,
Joyce quietly subverts this process by multiplying cases of
the feminine or rendering her image as mobile. At one point
in Stephen's revery there occurs the phrase 'ellipsoidal fall',
an echo of a ribald comment in a physics lecture. The
adjective is unusual enough to catch the reader's eye and
therefore functions as a reminder of a more profane context.
It is only a detail, but one of many which suggest a more
robust attitude to the real than Stephen's. Instead of
focusing on aesthetic product the novel enacts process, a
dialectic between the imagination and the self's context
which never stops, scarcely even pauses after the end of the

villanelle, where the birds' cries in the next scene echo those within the poem. The point is not, then, whether the villanelle represents a 'wet dream' (Kenner) or 'genuine inspiration' (Scholes) but rather how it functions dramatically within the development of Stephen's imagination. In *Stephen Hero* his poetry is explicitly linked with decadence and symbolism and his literary ambitions are soundly mocked: 'Stephen had now completed a series of hymns in honour of extravagant beauty and these he published privately in a manuscript edition of one copy' (*SH*, 219). In the earlier novel the villanelle is triggered by a chance event Stephen happens to witness, whereas in *A Portrait* Joyce pursues the psychological implications of the poem further. The villanelle relates to the brief prose poems – some, but not all, based on Joyce's original epiphanies – which together with composed and remembered poems all centre on a half-expressed languor (permutations of 'weary' form one of the most obvious motifs here). By the end of the novel Stephen has turned his back on this style; a night-time revery is dismissed as 'vague words for a vague emotion'.

The narrative of the villanelle's composition, as John Paul Riquelme has pointed out, 'directs attention to the dual status of writing as simultaneously product and process'.[15] He takes this as a central and self-reflexive section because it narrates the creation of the novel's text as well as Stephen's poem. What Riquelme does not discuss in his too close identification of Stephen with the narrator is the fact that the novel sets up opposing ways of reading the poem which bring its finality as product into question. Because the villanelle form depends so heavily on repetition it invites an internal reading which concentrates on the main critical question of how the poem disposes its repetitions while avoiding monotony. As with Dowson's poems, the words of Stephen's villanelle generate structure by their internal relations with each other. Against this reading we must recognise the poem's intertextual relation to other villanelles and the relation of its discourse to other nineteenth-century poems on the self and female other. There is a third reading possible, because the poem grows out of a narrative context. Bakhtin's insistence on words retaining the traces of earlier usage and earlier occurrences applies particularly well to the villanelle, where virtually every term comes charged with connotations which have accrued around its earlier appearance in the novel. To take only three examples from the first verse, 'weary' has become a privileged quality for Stephen in its special associations with beauty; 'fallen' carries a biographical echo of Stephen's mishap in the ditch at Clongowes, and then is developed during the retreat sermons to suggest a mythic prototype for Stephen; and 'teller' is established in Chapter 2 as a punning combination of commerce, literary expression and then religious observation ('telling' the rosary). *A Portrait* operates on a principle of complex verbal references backwards and forwards. A recognition of these echoes and anticipations is central to the meaning of the novel and such a reading of the villanelle denies it formal finality and deconstructs it back into its narrative matrix. Just as we become aware of the mobility of words' meanings, so Stephen develops a consciousness of their value as artistic raw material.

We shall see that Stephen becomes estranged from language for political reasons because he recognises the historical implications in using English. The aesthetic counterpart to this alienation is a realisation that words are plastic. The key passage occurs as Stephen is walking towards the seashore, where he experiences his bird–girl epiphany, and reads:

> – A day of dappled seaborne clouds.
> The phrase and the day and the scene harmonized in a chord. Words. Was it their colours? He allowed them to glow and fade, hue after hue: sunrise gold, the russet and green of apple orchards, azure of waves, the greyfringed fleece of clouds. No, it was not their colours: it was the poise and balance of the period itself. Did he then love the rhythmic rise and fall of

> words better than their associations of legend and colour? (*P*, 170)

The sequence is triggered by a phrase of summary description lifted out of context and recalled for its quality of evocation. Stephen's sense of harmony is explained as three monosyllables culminate in one ('chord'). Temporarily he becomes master of his vocabulary, but the sequence is articulated through alternations between questions and statements, so that Stephen is simultaneously experiencing a revery and trying to understand the sensuous appeal of language. His reflections on colour are orchestrated rhythmically ('glow and fade, hue after hue') so that the ultimate priority given to sound is implicit from the start, implicit in the iambic cadence of the quotation.

The two analogies raised here – language as colour, language as music – would have been Symbolist commonplaces by 1916. The latter found its most famous expression in Pater's adage that 'all art constantly aspires towards the condition of music', and Yeats, George Moore and the literary historian George Saintsbury all bore testimony to Pater's influence as the supreme master of prose cadence. Richard Ellmann has shown that Joyce incorporated Paterian phrasing into his essay on Mangan, and *A Portrait* contains many echoes of *Marius the Epicurean*, where the prose is finely tuned to evoke the intellectual development of the protagonist (E, 95). Joyce adapts Pater's musical emphasis in a number of different ways. At one point in *Stephen Hero* a prose poem linking dusk with decay is initiated by Stephen playing chords on a piano. Here the chords function simultaneously as metonym and metaphor of this harmony; in other words music functions as a relational device. In *A Portrait*, immediately prior to the passage quoted, Stephen seems to hear an 'elfin prelude', an accelerating and repeated phrase which can only be conveyed through analogy (like flames, like the pattering feet of running creatures) and which is again anchored to a prose quotation, this time from Newman. Here the musical phrase acts as a mysterious voice enticing Stephen forward towards an unknown future, and the quotation of the trigger-phrase releases new dimensions of connotation and suggestion.

Stephen Hero makes it quite explicit that Stephen's interest in words is derivative: 'He read Blake and Rimbaud on the values of letters and even permuted and combined the five vowels to construct cries for primitive emotions' (*SH*, 37). Rimbaud's 'Voyelles' similarly stands behind the speculations on the colour of words in *A Portrait*, but now Joyce shows Stephen's experiments at synaesthesia as attempts at verbal mastery. According to Arthur Symons, Rimbaud was constantly striving after an absolute meaning but only succeeding in producing a 'broken medley of fragments'.[16] A similar search for meaning lies behind the speculations which follow the completion of the villanelle. Standing on the steps of the library (an image which precedes as well as succeeds the composition of the poem), Stephen gazes at the birds flying around a 'temple of air'. The first term recalls Baudelaire's 'Correspondances' ('La Nature est un temple . . .'), which evokes a spatial expanse of potential meaning whose elusive unity tantalises the individual. C. P. Curran has recalled that 'correspondences, beginning with those that were the subject of Baudelaire's sonnet, always fascinated Joyce', and on the same page of *A Portrait* the narrative includes just such a correspondence from Swedenborg.[17] As in the last quoted passage from the novel this section moves forward by question and answer, and makes it clear that Stephen is attempting to read the scene for a concealed significance. He briefly thinks of 'Thoth, the god of writers, writing with a reed upon a tablet', imagining a primal script (partly signalled by his name) which has fixed his destiny (*P*, 229). Instead of locating himself within a tradition of artists, Stephen registers a panicky inability to stabilise meaning. The birds persist as cryptic signs and possible portents even while Stephen revises the image of Thoth into Dickensian caricature, naturalises his 'tablet' into a legal document and domesticates his name by noting its resemblance to an Irish oath.

In such areas of the novel we witness Stephen manoeuvring among earlier writers, convinced that literature will grant him access to truth. Here he remembers lines from Yeats's play *The Countess Cathleen* which evoke the poignancy of imminent departure through an analogy: 'as the swallow gazes / Upon the nest under the eave before / He wander the loud waters'. Stephen's preoccupation with cadence blinds him to the personal relevance of this quotation since it comes from the Countess's death speech after she has sold her soul. Locally, the lines contrast the fixity of the nest with the suggestion of expanse in 'waters', and the nest links analogically with home, temple and 'house of prayer'. The latter phrase is quoted by Christ when he casts the traders out of the temple. And so a nexus of contrasts is built up between interiors and exteriors, the piety of belonging as against the pathos of expulsion. Stephen evades these contrasts in favour of the immediate sensory appeal of Yeats's lines:

> A soft liquid joy like the noise of many waters flowed over his memory . . . . A soft liquid joy flowed through the words where the soft long vowels hurtled noiselessly and fell away, lapping and flowing back and ever shaking the white bells of their waves in mute chime and mute peal, and soft low swooning cry. (*P*, 230)

As usual, Stephen's thoughts include a quotation, this time from Psalm 93.iv: 'The Lord on high is mightier than the noise of many waters'. Just as Thoth's divinity is erased, so the deity stands behind this passage as an absence. The primary terms of the comparison in the passages from Yeats and the Bible are ignored in favour of the secondary figures which initiate a rhythmic incantatory sequence. The central notion of the sea supports a play of cadence where transference between the senses prevents any image from gelling. The bell–wave analogy works visually, but only because sound is blocked off by oxymorons ('mute peal').

A Reading of the Text

We are conscious, therefore, not only of rhythm but of erasure again, as if Stephen was suppressing memories. Indeed, this passage actually conflates echoes of Stephen's completion of the villanelle and of the seashore epiphany at the end of Chapter 4.

An important part of Stephen's struggle with language in the first chapter revolves around the question of verbal reference. Now this issue has taken on a heightened significance because Stephen has begun to understand the potential power of words. Haunted by semantic relativism, he turns to Swedenborg and the occult as substitute semiotic systems for the Catholicism he has lost. Even towards the end of the novel Stephen admits to Cranly his lingering respect for sacramental signs: 'I imagine . . . that there is a malevolent reality behind those things I say I fear' (*P*, 247). Without a supporting structure of signification these 'things' threaten and become symptomatic of a general problem confronting Stephen in language. His reveries and prose poems are constantly attempting to create internal areas of meaning (cadence, homophony, harmonisation, etc.), whereas the phrases and individual words he uses always come charged with previous associations. As the intertextual and *intra*textual echoes mount up, Stephen's word-paintings or tone poems recede into their narrative context and assume their places along the sequence of his experience. So in the passage just discussed the biblical phrases carry their own ironic reminder of the text and religious system Stephen is trying to escape; and the quotation from Yeats equally alerts us to the major Irish presence against which Stephen's artistic ambitions must define themselves.

It was during his discussion of the priesthood that Stephen was reminded of the power of words, since the priest's ability to bind and loose sins finds expression in ecclesiastical formulae. Stephen's rejection of that office involves a rejection of one verbal power for another, although a far more problematic one. Unlike Pater's Marius, Stephen does not experience a single moment of realisation, but his awareness of language grows throughout the novel. Marius, in contrast, reads Ovid's *Metamorphoses* and as a result becomes initiated into the 'secrets of utterance, of expression itself' which become an explicit replacement for more conventional prowess at military skills. Words for Marius 'were to be the apparatus of war for himself', although Pater overstates the former's antagonism towards the prevailing culture of Rome.[18] Stephen shows no such mixed feelings. His famous epigram ('Ireland is an old sow that eats her farrow') functions almost like an attempted exorcism of cultural pressures being exerted on him. He delivers this line 'with cold violence' and the Renaissance tropes of fencing and armed combat which pack this section of the novel reflect Stephen's perception of words as psychic and political weapons. This perception, however, only comes at the end of a prolonged struggle with language which persists throughout *A Portrait*.

4

Stephen's Dialogue with the Feminine

It very quickly becomes evident in the preceding section that Stephen's attempts at poetry cannot be discussed in isolation from his attitudes to women. The latter grow out of Catholicism, specifically out of the cult of the Virgin Mary, and polarise rival images of woman as saint and whore. In Chapter 3 we are told: 'the glories of Mary held his soul captive: spikenard and myrrh and frankincense, symbolizing her royal lineage, her emblems, the lateflowering plant and lateblossoming tree, symbolizing the agelong gradual growth of her cultus among men' (*P*, 108). To understand how this cult imprisons Stephen and how he tries to break free we need to identify a set of cultural associations lying at the centre of *A Portrait*.

The standard historical analysis of the cult of the Virgin Mary is Marina Warner's *Alone of All Her Sex* (1976), which documents the Church's assimilation of pagan religions and Aristotelian biology (the latter giving women the passive role of vessel in the process of procreation) into a tradition which enforced the 'association of sex, sin, and death'. The doctrine of the virgin birth became a sanction of chastity and the veneration of Mary as a queen made her a unique exception to the moral guilt of her sex since the church fathers from Augustine onwards held Eve responsible for the fall. The tenet of virginity took on further ramifications when the doctrine of the immaculate conception was formulated and spread, particularly by the Jesuits.

Within the iconography of the cult the moon was associated with fecunding dew sometimes referred to as 'moonwater', a detail which adds religious connotations to the opening of the villanelle episode in *A Portrait*. Warner concludes that there was a fundamental contradiction in the cult between motherhood and virginity: 'Mary establishes the child as the destiny of woman, but escapes the sexual intercourse necessary for all other women to fulfil this destiny.'[1] Towards the end of *A Portrait* Stephen overhears a servant singing and mentally transforms her into the 'figure of a woman as she appears in the liturgy of the church'. This involves forcing the figure back into childhood and even degendering her as 'a white-robed figure, small and slender as a boy' (*P*, 248).

The reason why such a figure is evoked emerges during Stephen's retreat, where the fall is recounted by one of the preachers. This account forms the expository centre of the novel since it presents the mythic origins of mankind's fallen nature and ultimately shows why, at the beginning of the chapter, Stephen should give primacy to lust as the origin of all the deadly sins. The preacher declares to the listening boys: 'The devil, once a shining angel, a son of the morning, now a foul fiend, came in the shape of a serpent, the subtlest of all the beasts of the field . . . . He came to the woman, the weaker vessel, and poured the poison of his eloquence into her ear' (*P*, 121). These lines skilfully conflate quotations from the Old Testament (Satan's original appearance), *King Lear* and Bunyan (the 'foul fiend'), Milton, the New Testament and *Hamlet* to suggest a common cultural inheritance prolonging the myth. The sermon is literally pieced together with excerpts from leading Western texts, which themselves quote from each other, so as to give a composite narrative of the fall. This narrative establishes exile and a consciousness of sin and death as the consequences of Eve's weakness. In *Stephen Hero* paradoxically it is the latter quality which attracts

Stephen: 'it was to Mary, as to a weaker and more engaging vessel of salvation, that he had trusted his spiritual affairs' (*SH*, 117). The preacher in *A Portrait* then introduces Mary as an anti-Eve, the 'virgin mother' whose son can reverse the results of the fall, but the main emphasis throughout the sermon lies, as we have seen, on punishment and guilt rather than redemption. The oxymoron of Mary's title creates an unresolved opposition between body and spirit which characterises Stephen's attitude to the opposite sex. Throughout the novel we will see him struggling for bearings between physical and spiritual images of femininity which prove to be ultimately irreconcilable.

The cult of the Virgin Mary was particularly strong in Victorian Ireland, especially after the 1879 visions of Knock, and it has also been argued by a social historian of the period that 'the Catholic clergy of the late nineteenth century and after were to become notorious for the rigid sexual morality which they imposed on their congregations.'[2] Fairly strong hints are given that Stephen's confessor at the end of Chapter 3 attaches a similar priority to his sexual wrongdoings. The *cause célèbre* of the 1890s where sexual misconduct had direct political consequences was, of course, the downfall of Parnell because of his liaison with Kitty O'Shea. Here we must return to the Christmas-dinner episode and read it afresh to see how its moral issues are involved with gender. Dante, one of Stephen's earliest teachers, carries the masculine name of the Italian poet who idealises the feminine, and is rumoured by Stephen's father to be a spoiled nun. She takes it upon herself to defend the Church from any criticism, answering historical specifics with assertions of principle and then, as the conversation degenerates into a slanging match, hurling abusive epithets and slogans at her male opponents. The centre of this argument, Mr Casey's story, gives an example of ignorant Irish 'piety' in the drunken old woman who screams against Kitty O'Shea (the Irish clergy regularly turned a blind eye to the evils of drink). First, she and then Dante repeat the clerical condemnation of Parnell but the episode lodges in Stephen's memory not only because ecclesiastical authority is questioned but because the old woman's term of abuse is not repeated. Sexual wrongdoing at this point becomes associated with verbal suppression and with non-verbal 'utterance'. Mr Casey spits on the woman to shut her up, inverting Christ's miracle of spitting on a blind man's eyes to restore his sight. The implications of parody, however, take second place to the traditional connotations of spitting as an act of mockery or defilement. It is introduced metaphorically as such by Dante, rendered literal by Mr Casey and almost repeated literally by Dante in the heat of her passion. She deindividualises Parnell as a devil to be conquered by the Church in one of a continuing series of struggles between absolute good and absolute evil, whereas Dedalus senior and Mr Casey bemoan the loss of an Irish leader. Joyce himself was sympathetic to this point of view, and in a series of notes he wrote for *Exiles* he remarked that the two greatest Irishmen of modern times – Swift and Parnell – 'broke their lives over women'.[3]

The Christmas argument does not conclude and the oppositions raised persist in Stephen's mind, taking on greater and greater proportions as the novel progresses. In 1903 Joyce had enthusiastically reviewed Marcelle Tinayre's novel *The House of Sin* for its depiction of a young man's struggle between sexual impulses and a strict Catholic upbringing. Joyce saw the novel as dealing with the problem of an uncompromising orthodoxy, beset by a peculiarly modern, or (as the Churchmen would say) 'morbid scepticism', and a similar tension gradually takes shape within Stephen (*CW*, 121). As Suzette Henke puts it, 'figuratively it is Stephen's ambition throughout the novel to "deflower" the Blessed Virgin of Catholicism. He wants to supplant the Catholic Madonna with a profane surrogate, an aesthetic muse rooted in sensuous reality.'[4] This may be what he wants, but it will be the burden of this section to show that Stephen never does escape the polarities imposed by the

Church and also that his struggle with these oppositions creates much of the novel's drama.

When Stephen visits Cork with his father he sees the word 'foetus' carved on a desk and is shocked by this sudden revelation of a tabooed vocabulary or physicality. The shock reflects an imbalance between Stephen's public discourse and a secret suppressed language of sexuality. By the end of the chapter he has begun to develop a façade of style and has separated his life into two distinct areas, each with their own psychological features. On the one hand there are Stephen's home and school, the places of decorum; and on the other hand, the squalid area of the Dublin brothels. A similarly stark contrast is established between the East and West ends of London in *The Picture of Dorian Gray* (a source for the descriptions which conclude Chapter 2 of *A Portrait*), where the protagonist's antitheses find articulation in his treatment of the allegorically named young actress Sybil Vane. From idealising her he swings violently round to an opposite recognition of her conventionality. A scene of high melodrama where each character voices the two opposing attitudes, marks their separation and leads first to Sibyl's death and then to the protagonist's. Dorian Gray casts himself as a respondent first to Sibyl's life-giving and then to her life-denying force, but it is his hand that finally takes his own life. Although he stands apart from the Catholic Church, Wilde explains his protagonist's actions in terms of a compulsion to sin and at such moments 'conscience is either killed, or, if it lives at all, lives but to give rebellion its fascination, and disobedience its charm.' And then Wilde anticipates Stephen's clerical instructors by adding: 'For all sins, as theologians weary not of reminding us, are sins of disobedience. When that high spirit, that morning-star of evil, fell from heaven, it was as a rebel that he fell.'[5] Dorian Gray dies because he can neither regress to the lost innocence of his childhood nor make an adequate confession of his sins.

The linguistic equivalent in *A Portrait* of Dorian Gray's

forays into the East End is a gradual displacement of lyricism by the suppressed language of lust. For Stephen this becomes an intensely physical process: 'The verses passed from his lips and the inarticulate cries and the unspoken brutal words rushed forth from his brain to force a passage' (*P*, 102). It is as if an automatic process is taking place and issues in sub-verbal sounds, suggesting that Stephen is nearer to animal life than humanity (moans, murmurs). Finally, a cry whose potential drama (and whose meaning) is denied by it being described as the echo of graffiti. Stephen has wandered into an area of noise not discourse. The only actual words given here are two brief invitations by a street walker and at the beginning of Chapter 3 the undifferentiated cries of the prostitutes appear as a collective solicitation and a collective example of jargon. One reason for this appears in *Stephen Hero*, when Stephen confides to Lynch that he does not consider prostitutes as human beings, giving as a typically scholastic justification the fact that the relevant Latin nouns are neuter. In *A Portrait* the young woman who takes Stephen into her room possesses a large doll with spreadeagled legs, which operates as a metonym of the woman's use to Stephen. By the Nighttown episode of *Ulysses* Joyce gives the prostitutes far greater verbal space so that they not only distinguish themselves from each other but also speak beyond their function.

The physical difficulties of expression Stephen experiences are presented as a hiatus between the signals of the brain and the organs of his body. Speech becomes internalised ('he tried to bid his tongue to speak') and the romantic trope of the love-look reappears here as a physical act of utterance with its response ('he read the meaning of her movements in her frank uplifted eyes'). Eyes, lips and tongue become the organs of erotic utterance in this immediate context, although elsewhere the tongue particularly takes on violently opposing connotations. The 'poison tongue' of Satan as serpent combines a quasi-phallic role with its originations of sin, whereas later in the novel Stephen mentions the hymn

'Pange Lingua Gloriosi' ('Sing my tongue, the glorious battle'). The different dimensions of meaning which the word takes on, whether sexual, reverential or penitential (the tongues of flame in Hell) reflect Stephen's shifting perceptions of linguistic utterance, since both in English and Latin the term puns on the physical organ and language as a whole. Joyce delighted in such puns because they united disparate and sometimes opposite meanings within the word, and a subdued tension runs through this episode as certain terms carry echoes of another more spiritual context. In the two phrases quoted at the beginning of this paragraph, for instance, 'uplifted' carries unmistakable suggestions of elevation and 'bid' simultaneously carries connotations of the Bible, instruction and prayer. Sure enough, in the next chapter we discover that Stephen leads the boys at Belvedere in reciting the devotional office to the Virgin Mary.

Suzette Henke has argued that for Stephen 'as a source of physical generation, woman serves as a reminder of animality, bodily decomposition, excrement, and death'; and she sees his final flight into exile as an attempt to escape from 'all the women who have served as catalysts in his own growth'.[6] She is certainly right to identify the persistent suggestion (again through a pun) of flight as an escape or an evasion, and she cogently glosses Stephen's reactions to women in individual terms. In producing an account of the novel's psychodynamics, however, she pays little attention to how far Stephen's reactions are determined by his cultural environment, or how far they involve his appropriation of the discourses of that environment. Stephen's attitudes to women are as volatile and shifting as his attitudes to art or to the Church, and the novel traces out a complex process of interaction between contrasting images.

In Chapter 3 the polar opposites of woman as saint and woman as sinner collide head on. Now the 'whores' are named as such and a startling conjunction takes place within sentences like the following:

> If ever his soul, re-entering her dwelling shyly after the frenzy of his body's lust had spent itself, was turned towards her whose emblem is the morning star, *bright and musical, telling of heaven and infusing peace*, it was when her names were murmured softly by lips whereon there still lingered foul and shameful words, the savour itself of a lewd kiss. (*P*, 108; Joyce's italics)

Stephen allegorises his physical return to his home as the re-entry of his soul into his body; in other words, he weaves a variation on a traditional example of Christian iconography. This implies that his sexual escapades involve an absence or voiding (in the Victorian slang meaning of 'spent') and a recognition of sin even before the retreat starts. The spiritual is identified as feminine whereas the body – initially at least – is masculine. Midway through the sentence the narrative past shifts into the present tense and ushers in a quotation from Newman's discourse on the Virgin Mary. By positioning the passage here Joyce associates correct reverence with return, and through obvious contrasts (morning and night, brightness and darkness, etc.) concisely presents Stephen's physical actions as an opposition to a key emblem and, by implication, to the Church itself. Mary's name is elided in favour of an area of reference, a set of terms which in the final climactic section of this sentence tug against their profane opposites. When the full passage from Newman is quoted later in the chapter it becomes evident that Stephen was suppressing phrases which would highlight this contrast: 'thy very face and form, dear mother, speak to us of the Eternal' and her emblem as the morning star 'breathes' purity (*P*, 142). The virgin's image is every bit as eloquent as the prostitute's face we were just considering. All the former's emblems *tell* of heaven. They address Stephen, whose lips now become the site of a verbal and moral conflict as he finds himself unable to reconcile the fact that agape and eros are articulated through the same organ of expression. At this point in the novel love becomes a principle of divinely sanctioned order, whereas sexuality is figured as an anarchic subversive force, even an illness with its own 'fever'. From the very beginning he was more comfortable with distinctions than with identities, and here, unable to resolve two images and two opposing images, he falls back on a childhood formulation of puzzlement: 'It was strange.'

The whole point of the novel is that it is not strange at all for such a conflict to occur given Stephen's upbringing and the historical moment of his adolescence. The sentence discussed leaves it ambiguous how many words emerge from Stephen's thoughts and how many are an external articulation by the narrator; and this ambiguity recurs throughout the novel because Stephen's capacity to assimilate the discourse of others undermines this internal/external distinction. Many passages read like external narrative comment precisely because so much of Stephen's consciousness assembles quotations. We have seen that a large part of his education consists of learning by rote and so it is appropriate for his thoughts on women to develop out of the phrases learnt from the Litany of the Virgin Mary. Like Dorian Gray's Sybil, the first girl to lodge in Stephen's memory has hands like ivory. Whereas in Wilde's novel the comparison is a romantic cliché, Stephen's thoughts about Eileen Vance are inseparable from the phrase 'tower of ivory', which itself derives from an erotic catalogue in the Song of Songs. In trying to understand the phrase Stephen draws a distinction (it is unavailable to Protestants) and a physical association with the touch of Eileen's hands. Paradoxically, as he moves towards understanding, Stephen secularises the notion of ivory, charging it with sexual connotations and gender difference (Eileen tells him what a strange thing it is to have pockets). Nevertheless the term 'ivory' retains its spiritual implications so that the simple fact of its recurrence in the seashore epiphany signals a reverential attitude on Stephen's part to the image before him.

A similar process of elaboration and retention takes place with other phrases from the Litany: 'house of gold', 'mystical rose', 'morning star', 'refuge of sinners'. Each of these expressions embeds itself in Stephen's consciousness and is developed through different contexts. The emblems might overlap. We have just seen the association between the Virgin and the figure of the house. Newman's discourse also identifies her with the Church itself and so a set of associations is built up between 'house', 'refuge' and the place of true faith. As Chapter 3 progresses the Virgin Mary assumes an explicitly central position for Stephen and her full texts are gradually admitted by him for utterance. So at the beginning we recognise fragmentary quotations; before the last sermon these quotations are organised into prayer but given in indirect speech; finally, Newman's text (itself an application of the Litany) is given directly and as a prayer. In a fantasy of the Virgin Mary performing a sexless betrothal of Stephen to Emma, of whom more in a moment, Mary speaks directly to their hearts, and one of the main progressions in Chapter 3 is from suppressed utterance to verbal relief. Stephen's secret written 'confessions' are misnamed because they are concealed erotic fictions, whereas the whole push of the chapter is 'to say it in words'. Even Stephen's nightmare of goatlike beings (monstrous versions of his own lust) envisages a kind of verbal excretion ('soft language issued from their spittleless lips') which triggers his own physical voiding (nausea) and then the spiritual purgation of confession. This confession involves a ritual procedure, and one measure of the change that has taken place in Stephen is the difference between him reading prayers 'in a veiled voice' at the beginning of the chapter and the total absence of ironic qualification in 'he prayed'.

The suggestion of equilibrium at the end of Chapter 3 is deceptive because, as Hugh Kenner has rightly warned us, the balance of the chapter-endings always acts as a prelude to fresh disruptions. Stephen appears to have stilled the voice of the flesh and to have allowed idealistic images of femininity to assume priority over their profane counter-parts. We do not, however, need to go very far into the next chapter before an inner dialogue masquerading as prayer and response reasserts itself: 'An inaudible voice seemed to caress the soul, telling her names and glories, bidding her arise as for espousal and come away, bidding her look forth, a spouse, from Amana and from the mountains of the leopards; and the soul seemed to answer with the same inaudible voice, surrendering herself: *Inter ubera mea commorabitur*' (*P*, 155). The opening oxymoron displaces utterance from the voice to physical gesture and transposes litanic recital into an internalised and narcissistic devotion to another part of the self. As so often happens with Stephen's thoughts, mental sequence gives way quickly to pastiche and quotation, this time from the Song of Songs, which served as a source for his cherished phrase 'tower of ivory'. The dialogue which takes place in that book between male and female voices expresses a direct erotic desire which has been partially idealised by Stephen's intermediary text, a Jesuit devotional work. But the erotic dimension has by no means been filtered out. On the contrary the quotation from the Song of Songs 1.xiii ('he shall lie all night betwixt my breasts') stands out typographically and linguistically from its surrounding context. Stephen appears to be performing an act of orthodoxy by quoting from the Bible, but the erotic content of the passage undermines its apparent piety. The 'inaudible voice' (which partly echoes the 'inarticulate cries' of the flesh at the end of Chapter 2) enacts a sexual engagement between male and female poles of the self, in effect the one attempting a verbal seduction of the other. One interpretation of the Song of Songs defuses its sexuality by taking it as a prediction of Christ's love for the Church, but Stephen, as it were, works backwards from the Litany of the Virgin Mary to the unavoidable physicality of the earlier book. Within this local context it is impossible to take Stephen's 'ejaculations' as denoting only short prayers. The whole passage just quoted is full of uncertainties and unresolved ambiguities. Are the voices referred to one and the same, in which case how can a dialogue be taking place? Are the voices inaudible because Stephen is trying to suppress any reminder of his own physicality? The repetition of 'seemed' functions as a traditional enough signal of a margin of error. In short, the internalised observation of religious form proves to be shot through with implications which render its piety suspect. We have by now grown used to Stephen's evocation of the flesh as a voice whose utterances are often smothered, and even when he is questioned about the priesthood he immediately thinks of that office in erotic terms, as granting him special access to *female* confessions of sin. Here we need to pause to consider the role in *A Portrait* of one of the few female characters in the novel who is given a name and a substantial role to play – Emma Clery. A brief contrast with her appearance in *Stephen Hero* will clarify her function in the later novel.

Emma startles Stephen by her lively interest in a range of topics, which he defensively rationalises as a 'distressing pertness'. In their passage of dialogue, except for their last meeting, she takes the initiative in asking Stephen questions about himself. This happens one evening as they cross Stephen's Green, a haunt for courting couples:

> A feminine voice called out from the dusky region of the couples 'Don't!'
> – Don't, said Emma. Isn't that Mr Punch's advice to young men who are about to marry . . . . I hear you are quite a woman-hater now, Stephen.
> – Wouldn't that be a change?
> – And I heard you read a dreadful paper in the college – all kinds of ideas in it. Isn't that so?
> – Please don't mention that paper.
> – But I'm sure you're a woman-hater. You've got so stand-offish, you know, so reserved. Perhaps you don't like ladies' company?
> Stephen pressed her arm a little by way of a disclaimer.
> – Are you a believer in the emancipation of women too? she asked.
> – To be sure! said Stephen. (*SH*, 158)

The monosyllable from the dusk is incorporated by Emma into their conversation about marriage as she tries to confront Stephen with his growing reputation as a non-conformist. He shuts off the taboo subject of his paper on aesthetics and keeps the dialogue on a different theoretical level, but under the surface of their words is running a flirtatious sub-text introduced by the sexual implications of the overheard call. Emma asks about Stephen's attitude in general while tacitly questioning him about his behaviour towards herself. It is important to note not only his laconic replies but also the eloquence of physical gesture. Once Stephen takes over the initiative and asks her about confession, her body gives an affirmative response while she states a decorous warning: 'She leaned a little more appreciably on his arm and said: "Now don't be bold, Stephen"' (*SH*, 159). In fact, Stephen has only picked up a conversational cue from her when she suggests that feminism is the only true faith and shifted the analogy round to create a new intimacy between them.

Instead of enjoying this intimacy Stephen registers annoyance with the casual hypocrisy of their conversation and later tries to force a closure of the gap between words and feeling – with laughable results. His friend Lynch diagnoses temporary insanity in Stephen's attempt to break through social restraint but a gloss on the manuscript of the novel (Joyce's?) explains: 'Stephen wishes to avenge himself on Irish women who, he says, are the cause of all the moral suicide in the island' (*SH*, 205). This gloss is a dramatic one, giving an internal account of Stephen's actions according to his own perspective, whereas the novel constantly invites us to view him from the outside – the conversation with Lynch does exactly that. With the benefit of this less flattering viewpoint Stephen's erotic invitation to Emma could be read as a disingenuous means of forcing a break with an opposing and intractable presence.

Emma's relation to Stephen is described within the means of social realism, whereas *A Portrait* positions her along a series of images of the feminine which begin with Eileen and which continue with the 'impalpable' form of Mercedes, whom Stephen dreams of encountering after reading Dumas. This 'tryst', this secret meeting-place where male and female will emerge, operates as the focus of a yearning kept alive by repeating the name Mercedes to himself. Like the boy-narrator of 'Araby' in *Dubliners* who creates a cherished religiose image of Mangan's sister (the character is deliberately named after the poet of romantic idealism) amid the banal life of Dublin, Stephen dreams of a female form whose identity is kept carefully vague. Similarly, although Emma is a more actualised presence in the novel, she too is distanced by Stephen and can only be distinguished from other female figures with difficulty because she is rarely named. One of her most substantial descriptions occurs at a leave-taking after a party when they stand in the entrance to a tram, apparently overheard by the horses:

> They seemed to listen, he on the upper step and she on the lower. She came up to his step many times and went down to hers again between their phrases and once or twice stood close beside him for some moments on the upper step, forgetting to go down, and then went down. His heart danced upon her movements like a cork upon a tide. He heard what her eyes said to him from beneath their cowl and knew that in some dim past, whether in life or in revery, he had heard their tale before. He saw her urge her vanities, her fine dress and sash and long black stockings, and knew that he had yielded to them a thousand times. Yet a voice within spoke above the noise of his dancing heart, asking him would he take her gift to which he had only to stretch out his hand. (*P*, 71)

Although a verbal exchange is taking place, the passage relies for its effect on a meta-dialogue between the two characters' bodies. Stephen stays physically immobile while the girl moves to and fro balletically miming out a flirtatious invitation. He sententiously condemns the very things which are appealing to him as 'vanities' (in the scriptural sense of being empty) perhaps because he has yielded to them before. His immobility represents a proud holding back from the 'words' of her eyes but the passage also suggests a disparity between head and heart, between fixity and animated internal motion. Indeed, the real event here seems to be taking place within Stephen's psyche as an encounter between the 'noise' of his heart and a more lucid voice asking a question.

This question is not answered and lapses because to Stephen Emma can only be perceived as an image which repeatedly contrasts unfavourably with her actual behaviour. Earlier in Chapter 2 he rejects her manner as silly and after the 'last tram' episode he can only begin a poem to the girl by erasing her name to initials. It is only when Stephen has abstracted the suitable qualities from the original scene that the two lovers can kiss. We shall see that this aesthetic idealisation can only take place within the safe bounds of his poem, whereas the to-and-fro movement of Emma in the quoted passage repeats itself throughout the second half of the novel in a series of meetings and departures. In Chapter 3 Stephen registers a consciousness of having defiled Emma's image in a kind of mental rape which brings his literary idealism under heavy pressure: 'Was that chivalry? Was that poetry?' (*P*, 119). The questions cannot be answered but the novel has already indicated the linkage perceived by Stephen when the prostitute's facial expression at the end of the preceding chapter is presented as a more overt but basically identical invitation to Emma's. The descriptive detail in the paragraph quoted above that Emma's head is cowled in effect factures her image between the sacred and the profane because the cowl as an item of monastic or clerical dress is repeatedly associated with the Church. It is thus a very relevant detail that he should register intense jealousy when she becomes the object of a *priest's* attentions in their Gaelic class. Towards the end of *A Portrait* Emma questions Stephen about his artistic ambitions without realising that her image has been caught up within those ambitions. It is no accident that the composition of different sections of the villanelle frames a memory of Emma. The origins of this idealising impulse can be traced back ultimately to the cult of the Virgin Mary.

Later in the novel a fresh memory of Emma emerges which recapitulates her eloquent movement from the 'last tram' episode. Briefly, she actualises details from Stephen's revery (white flower, glowing cheek) but then dances away from him. The lengthy conversation which occurs between the two in *Stephen Hero* is now condensed into four terse lines of speech which tantalisingly hint at a series of previous contacts between Stephen and Emma which have not been narrated:

– You are a great stranger now.
– Yes, I was born to be a monk.
– I am afraid you are a heretic.
– Are you much afraid? (*P*, 224)

Almost in shorthand, with no distracting reference to tone or gesture, these words function as reminders of important themes: Stephen's sense of purpose, his relation to orthodoxy, his position within his community. No sooner has Stephen used the term 'monk' than he figures himself as a Franciscan heretic (i.e. ambivalently neither inside nor outside the Church) whispering into Emma's ear. For a second he reverts to a satanic proto-type seducing Eve and later in the same episode expresses awareness mythically as post-lapsarian nostalgia for lost innocence. Stephen once again fails to stabilise his sense of Emma, wavering between 'homage' and a sad recognition of the 'dark shame of womanhood'. It is physical maturation which supposedly stimulates this 'shame' and the terms 'sin' and 'innocence' continue to dance around each other at this point. They reflect in turn an unresolved alternation of attitude between idealistic respect and a desire to corrupt. Each of these attitudes, of course, suggests that Stephen is attempting to slot Emma into the role of virgin or fallen woman, but right to the very end of the novel she eludes this introjection by persisting as another voice in her own right.

The one female figure whom we have not considered so far is in some ways the most important – Stephen's mother. The cult of the Virgin Mary celebrates an apotheosis of motherhood which feeds directly into Joyce's Epiphany 34, which describes a spiritual visitation from this 'mother most venerable' (a significant revision of the litanic phrase 'virgin most venerable').[7] This figure combines physical and spiritual principles of love ('years and years I loved you when you lay in my womb') which, as we shall see in a moment, is a vital issue in Joyce's fiction. We might logically expect Stephen's mother to be contrasted with the fathers who populate *A Portrait* because they represent a collective source of opposition. Edmund L. Epstein's monograph, *The Ordeal of Stephen Dedalus* (1971), documents the argument that fathers in Joyce have as a purpose the thwarting of sons and particularly the thwarting of filial rebellion. Simon Dedalus, the Jesuit clerics and even the czar represent forms of authority which Stephen is trying to subvert. We have already seen examples of the discourse involved in this opposition. Mary Dedalus – her forename's significance is obvious – functions in quite a different way.

In *Stephen Hero* Mrs Dedalus is a personification of middle-class decency, but she does show an interest in Stephen's reading. Their conversation about Ibsen raises the issues of artistic subjects (should these things be talked about?), an idealistic aesthetic (should art provide uplift?) and the pathos of the mother's subjection to the father. In fact, subjection becomes foregrounded and identified as social coercion when Stephen tries to define himself against his sister, who 'acquiesces in the religion of her mother'. Both literature and the Church are discussed as social institutions in the two main conversations Stephen has with his mother, and a sharp irony emerges from their exchange over the former's loss of faith when his mother seems to be more preoccupied by the social disgrace than by the fate of Stephen's soul. His questions to his mother put pressure on two areas vulnerable to logic – the miracles and the accretions of tradition – but in a sense they are details because Stephen is all too aware of the priests and organisation standing behind his mother. For that reason he depersonalises their argument to a friend as a clash 'with orthodoxy'.

In *A Portrait* Stephen's mother is a less vocal but more important presence. She is the first and last female character in the novel, and the early details referring to her give no real indication of the symbolic force she will assume. She emerges initially as a form of physical comfort to Stephen and also as the promoter of verbal taboos. All her instructions to Stephen are negative (not to use certain words, not to speak to rough boys, etc.), just as she tries to act as a peacemaker at the Christmas dinner table by asking her guests not to discuss politics. Mrs Dedalus then recedes into the hinterland of the novel until a discussion between Stephen and Cranly transforms her into an issue: the nature of maternal love. Where the conversation about Stephen's loss of faith is given directly in *Stephen Hero*, it is reported through a later exchange in *A Portrait*. This change shifts the focal issue from 'decent' hypocrisy as honest doubt to love, and Cranly becomes an advocate for the rights Stephen's mother would never claim. Insisting on the ultimate authenticity of maternal feelings, he rejects the authoritative gynophobic statements by Pascal and others which Stephen quotes to him. Chapter 5 of *A Portrait* conceptualises many of the novel's earlier themes as abstract issues – female beauty is one such topic – but Cranly simply shouts down the stated positions as if to reveal an imbalance within Stephen between a hypertrophied intellect and atrophied feelings. Following a discussion about the Virgin Mary with his mother, the diary section virtually concludes with the latter praying that Stephen may learn 'what the heart is'. Given his position in the Sodality of the Blessed Virgin at Belvedere College, it is ironic that Stephen does not pay more attention to his own mother.

For the full implications of his indifference to emerge we

have to wait until *Ulysses*. Here Buck Mulligan takes over Cranly's interrogatory role and diagnoses Stephen's refusal to pray at his mother's deathbed as a sign of a 'cursed Jesuit strain'. In the Nighttown episode the prostitute Florry comes to the conclusion that Stephen is a 'spoiled priest or monk', neatly inverting Simon Dedalus' aspersion about Dante. Stephen's mother acts as a submerged psychological presence throughout the novel until she finally rises from the grave to her son's horror 'uttering a silent word'. The publication in 1984 of the definitive text of *Ulysses* has confirmed that this was 'love', the 'word known to all men', and it is through the conversation between Stephen and Cranly that the term is most prominently foregrounded in *A Portrait*.

5

Stephen Dedalus' Languages

In the preceding sections we have seen how issues of authority, religion, aesthetics and gender return constantly to issues of verbal expression, and language itself constantly occupies the novel's foreground. Stephen Dedalus is born into a country where the native language has been superseded by an imperial one. His schooling centres importantly on learning Latin, the language of the classics and of the Church. At university he begins to study French and Italian, which rival Gaelic as the languages of culture. The result is that episodes are repeatedly drawing attention to linguistic transactions; the new 'worlds' which Stephen enters are to a large extent new areas of discourse with their own idioms; and when he dreams of escaping to the Continent its glamour is figured linguistically ('Europe of strange tongues'). From entire languages through dialects, sociolects and even comic idiolects like Lynch's use of 'yellow' (cf. Cranly's use of 'oracle' in *Stephen Hero*) *A Portrait* dramatises the complexity and heterogeneity of discourse. No account of how Stephen passes from one experience to another can afford to ignore this since, as Michael Bernard-Donals has pointed out, 'language is not a process of separation of selves. Rather, it is a way of overcoming the separation of selves by way of negotiating a social place in the world.'[1] The languages of the novel in short offer Stephen means of situating himself.

Latin in *A Portrait* is the privileged language of ritual and the sacred, and because it is used by Stephen's clerical mentors it also becomes the language of discipline. The first mention of Latin is a schoolboy joke about Caesar's 'calico belly' which hinges on the intersection between two languages, and towards the end of the novel Stephen looks back on the awkwardly stylised English which came out of the boys' translations of Ovid and Horace. At this stage he can register a cool detachment over these translations, but in Chapter 1 there is a close continuity between the grammatical rules of Latin and the discipline of Clongowes. A failure to decline a Latin noun leads to one boy being punished and to Stephen's beating, and the hated sign of this discipline (the pandybat) includes within its title the order which goes with its use: 'pande', i.e. 'hold out'. The beating is an early and crudely physical example of the discipline of the Church. Joyce also draws out the 'enormous, highly specialized methodological apparatus . . . for transmitting and interpreting various kinds of holy word', which Bakhtin finds to be characteristic of religious systems (*DI*, 351). Recital is one favoured means; thus Stephen reads out the order of the Virgin Mary 'in a veiled voice'. The repetitions of prayer and spiritual responses to the words of the mass supply other examples of the stylised use of Latin and, as we shall see, of the Church's disciplined voices.

It is, however, a principle of discourse in *A Portrait* that no single mode is privileged over others. On a much smaller scale the novel anticipates the decentred discourse of *Ulysses* in that respect. The decorum of Church Latin is no exception, because as early as Chapter 2 Stephen facetiously recites the *Confiteor* and in his late conversation with Cranly screens the intimacy of his admissions by stylising them as a confession. The Latin language itself becomes a butt for the students' humour. Bakhtin has noted that medieval travesties of Latin included with their 'serious and rather subtle grammatical analysis . . . a sharp parodic exaggeration of this very subtlety, and of the scrupulousness of scholarly analysis' (*DI*, 73). On a less sophisticated level, the Dublin students' grafting of English on to Latin displays an irreverence to the grammar of either language and mocks the scholarly solemnity which goes with their official usages. So Temple's sole philological comment to Stephen characteristically takes place outside the lecture room and with reference to a profanity – 'ballocks' – as a survival of the dual number. Stephen himself uses a different tactic at university. Instead of mocking the method of linguistic scholarship, as Umberto Eco has pointed out, 'Stephen conceals with casuist ability, under medieval garments' propositions which the clerics cannot question because they fall 'victims of their own traditional formalism in which the words of the Doctor Angelicus (i.e. Thomas Aquinas) could not be discussed'.[2] Stephen's quotations from Aquinas are quietly subversive because they preserve the decorum of ecclesiastical citation while using them to promote secular aesthetic propositions.

Bakhtin explains that the novel comes into being by dispersing ideology among the different forms of language available at any given historical moment. 'It is a consciousness', he continues, 'manifesting itself in the midst of social languages that are surrounded by a single (national) language, and in the midst of (other) national languages that are surrounded by a single culture' (*DI*, 367). Bakhtin cites as one example the Roman Empire, but it would be far more useful to bear in mind the British imperial context in relation to *A Portrait*. At the turn of the century the question of a national language for Ireland had become a subject for heated debate. Douglas Hyde, founder of the Gaelic League in 1893 and tireless promoter of the National Literary Society, called in 1892 for his compatriots to purge themselves of the oppressive cultural influence of England. The first step lay in the language itself: 'In order to de-Anglicize ourselves we must at once arrest the decay of the language .... We must arouse some spark of patriotic inspiration among the peasantry who still use the language.'[3] Hyde demanded nothing short of a cultural boycott of England, but W. B. Yeats was uneasy. In December of

1892 he wrote a letter of response to the periodical *United Ireland* expressing the desire for a middle path:

> Can we not keep the continuity of the nation's life, not by trying to do what Dr. Hyde has practically pronounced impossible, but by translating or retelling in English, which shall have an indefinable Irish quality of rhythm and style, all that is best of the ancient literature?[4]

The battle-lines were thus drawn up in the 1890s between those nationalists who wanted to pursue the cause of Gaelic and those who sought an Irish form of English. The attraction of the former was partly symbolic because Hyde was determined once and for all to end what he perceived as a sense of shame in the Irish when using their own tongue.

Joyce himself could hardly avoid getting caught up in this debate. His fellow student George Clancy (the model for Davin in *A Portrait*) helped to found a branch of the Gaelic League at University College and persuaded Joyce to take Gaelic lessons 'for a year or two'.[5] Among his teachers was Patrick Pearse, later to be executed after the Easter Uprising of 1916. These Gaelic lessons figure prominently in *Stephen Hero* as occasions for demonstrating the confusions in Stephen's thinking about rebellion. He more or less gives up an argument about the political necessity of Gaelic and limits his commitment to the lessons by refusing to pay his subscription to the League. Similarly, when he listens to patriotic Irish poetry he filters out the sentiments and wilfully notes only the use of certain verbal contractions. The grammar lessons are described as a substitute for political oratory: the teacher 'never lost an opportunity of sneering at seoninism (i.e. West Britonism, the belief in Irish allegiance to England) and at those who would not learn their native tongue. He said that Beurla [i.e. the English language] was the language of commerce and Irish the speech of the soul' (*SH*, 64). This elevated claim juxtaposes ironically with Joyce's description of a clique centring on a 'very stout black-bearded citizen' who holds court in a Dublin tobacco-shop. This figure is named in *A Portrait* as

Michael Cusack, the founder of the Gaelic Athletic Association, and is later parodied at length as the Citizen in the Cyclops episode of *Ulysses*.

Before we examine how Gaelic figures in *A Portrait* an intermediary text needs to be considered: namely, a lecture which Joyce delivered on Ireland in Trieste in 1907. 'Ireland, island of saints and sages' stresses the ancient pedigree of Gaelic and discusses its revival without a shade of irony: 'The Irish language . . . has an alphabet of special characters, and a history almost three thousand years old . . . . Now the Gaelic League has revived its use . . . . In the streets, you often see groups of young people pass by speaking Irish' (*CW*, 155–6). Joyce's respect for the language was reinforced by the symbolic importance he attached to the Book of Kells which offered him a model of artistic construction, and he later was to incorporate many Gaelic words into *Finnegan's Wake*. However, Joyce's tacit recognition of the dignity of Gaelic did not blind him to the actual state of affairs in Ireland. The 1907 lecture gives a thumbnail sketch of Irish history and concludes that, given the mixed nature of its civilisation, it is futile to expect purity: 'What race, or what language . . . can boast of being pure today? . . . Nationality . . . must find its reason for being rooted in something that surpasses and transcends and informs changing things like blood and the human word' (*CW*, 165–6). These sentiments must have gone down well with the polyglot audiences of Trieste and by following a rather different historical route Joyce arrives at a position similar to Bakhtin's: that the linguistic situation in Ireland was heterogeneous and historically diverse.

The question of whether or not to learn Gaelic is an oddly diminished issue in *A Portrait*. Now Joyce focuses it on Stephen's relation to his fellow student Davin and uses the latter as a figure of contrast. Davin's willingness to learn Gaelic is presented as intellectual docility: 'Davin had sat at the feet of Michael Cusack . . . . His nurse had taught him Irish and shaped his rude imagination by the broken lights of Irish myth' (*P*, 184). Gaelic is reduced to a few Fenian watchwords which Stephen delights to repeat in mockery, and Davin is categorised as a 'dull-witted loyal serf', a personification of the acquiescence from which Stephen is recoiling. He is therefore dominated rhetorically by a set of terms ('serf', 'serve', etc.) which carry heavily pejorative connotations, and he even falls victim to his own cherished Irish myths when Stephen casts himself as an intellectual Milesian addressing Davin as a primitive Firbolg, that is, a cultural primitive.

When Davin speaks he immediately becomes a more forceful figure in the novel because he emerges as a narrator in his own right and because his speech demonstrates rhythms which are unavailable to Stephen. Here we encounter the third main alternative to 'standard' English in *A Portrait*, namely Anglo-Irish or, as it is now called, Hiberno-English. In contrast with *Stephen Hero*, the later novel grants far more space to varieties of the vernacular, and the examples which follow all revolve around speech. Joyce's source-book for this area of the novel was P. W. Joyce's *English as we Speak it in Ireland* (1910), a work which he also drew on for *Ulysses*. Joyce's namesake was the President of the Royal Society of Antiquaries in Ireland from 1906 to 1908 and wrote a number of books on Irish topics including *The Origin and History of Irish Names of Places*, to which Joyce refers in his broadside ballad 'Gas from a burner'. *English as we Speak it* falls into two parts. The first gives examples of general characteristics of style, while the second gives a glossary of the dialect. As usual in *A Portrait* it is not until late in the novel that Anglo-Irish idioms become an explicit subject for comment, but Joyce introduces his examples much earlier.

There are three passages of dialogue in *A Portrait* which supply the relevant data: the Christmas-dinner argument, the conversation between Stephen's father and his associates in Cork, and conversations between Davin, Cranly and Stephen in Chapter 5. Stephen's father's idiolect contains within it many of the stylistic features which P. W. Joyce demonstrates through example. Dedalus senior is the first named speaker in the novel and it is therefore appropriate for him to personify a national idiom. He typically uses mild profanities ('bedad'), quotes maxims ('you must put your shoulder to the wheel'), uses physical analogies ('fed up . . . like gamecocks') and a whole range of emphatic devices ('by God', 'Holy Paul', etc.) which ironically contradict P. W. Joyce's assertion that 'the general run of our people do not swear much'.[6] The contrasts between himself and his son figure constantly as differences between a self-consciously vigorous oral idiom and written styles of English. As Joyce himself put it, 'the Dubliner passes his time gabbing and making the rounds in bars', and Simon Dedalus sums up this characteristic with a vengeance (E, 217). He sets up Mr Casey's story over the Christmas dinner table and the latter goes through a careful ritual of delivery, pacing himself so as to whet his audience's curiosity. First, he introduces his tale, situates it ('down in Arklow') and then pauses out of respect for the dead 'chief' (i.e. Parnell). When he launches on the story proper he uses emphatic inversion ('such hooing and haaing, man, you never heard') and augmented repetition ('well there was one old lady, and a drunken old harridan she was surely'). His asides, his pauses for effect and his skill at mimicry build up to the punch-line of his story, which combines physical movement and a skill in adjusting his tone of voice. This miniature masterpiece of delivery is aggressively secular in purpose and outrages Dante as a protector of the Church's solemn discourse.

In the above scene Stephen functions as a witness but on his visit to Cork his rapid disenchantment with the 'lively southern speech' results in a foregrounding of the latter's idiom. When Stephen and his father eat 'drisheens' for breakfast the term acts as stylistic signal that they have entered another area of discourse. P. W. Joyce glosses the pudding in the following way: 'this viand and its name are peculiar to Cork, where *drisheen* is considered suitable for persons of weak or delicate digestion.'[7] Essentially, Simon Dedalus is trying to regain acceptance into the community of Cork, which he does by dismissing Stephen as a 'jackeen' (i.e. a conceited citizen of Dublin). When he finally discovers a former crony Dedalus senior engages in a dialogue where dialect usages are cues for agreement and solidarity. The laboured intimacy within the dialogue contrasts with the repetitive formality with which Joyce designates the two speakers ('Mr. Dedalus' and 'the little old man') so that the reader (like Stephen) becomes distanced from their words. Accordingly, we pay more attention to the tactics of the conversation, which thrives on repetition.

> – Now don't be putting ideas into his head, said Mr. Dedalus. Leave him to his Maker.
> – Yerra, sure I wouldn't put any ideas into his head. (*P*, 97)

Mr Dedalus has described himself as trying to lose his Cork accent, but a reversion to, for instance, the continuous tense in the imperative leads to a response with 'an exclamation very much in use in South' meaning 'look out', an emphatic modifier equivalent to the English 'certainly', and a virtual repetition of Dedalus' words.[8] As the conversation proceeds redundancy becomes more and more obvious, and statement and response turn into a ritual every bit as stylised as an antiphon. That formality culminates in the last lines, where a routine expression of piety frames a revision of Dedalus' sentiment from minimalisation to its opposite:

> – And thanks be to God . . . that we lived so long and did so little harm.
> – Thanks be to God we lived so long and did so much good. (*P*, 98)

In the Cork episode Joyce uses dialect to draw out the degree of Stephen's alienation from the discourse. To a large extent this is caused by his exclusion from a closed circle of repetitions. The issue of belonging has lapsed, at least in this form, by the time we encounter Stephen's friend Davin. By this stage in the novel Stephen is willing to act as appreciative audience to a narrative with its own characteristic style, which starts with an extensive series of dialect forms, most of them here marked for clarity and most of them pieced together from P. W. Joyce:

> I was away all that day *from my own place* over in Buttevant.
> – I don't know if you know where that is – at a hurling match between the Croke's Own Boys and the Fearless Thurles and *by God*, Stevie, that was *the* hard fight. My first cousin, Fonsy Davin, was stripped *to his buff* that day *minding cool* for the Limericks but he was up with the forwards half the time and shouting like mad. I never will forget that day. One of the Crokes made a woeful *wipe* at him one time with his *camann* and *I declare to God* he was within an *aim's ace* of getting it at the side of the temple. Oh, *honest to God*, if the crook of it caught him that time he was done for. (*P*, 185)

Just like Mr Casey, Davin situates his narrative with a concessional aside to Stephen. The signs of oral address are naming his listener, exclaiming to him and introducing the game through the definite article as a superlative modifier. Joyce is careful to choose vocabulary either specific to Munster ('to his buff', 'minding cool' – i.e. goal) or general to Ireland as a whole like 'wipe' (i.e. a blow, as from a 'camaun' or hurley-stick). 'Aim's ace' (standard usage would omit the first word) is explained by P. W. Joyce as 'a survival . . . of the old Shakesperian word *ambs-ace* or two single points in throwing dice'.[9] Davin interjects comments within his narrative to stress his excitement. He uses repetition ('one . . . one') and alliteration ('woeful wipe' perhaps suggested by the Ulster expression 'goaly-wipe') to catch the moment-by-moment drama of the event; and he invokes God as a pious declaration of narrative credentials.

Although Stephen has no time for Davin's beliefs, nevertheless as a connoisseur of styles he cherishes the latter's speech. Its distinction from the other registers we have met does not compare at all well with Stephen's other friend Cranly: 'Cranly's speech, unlike that of Davin, had neither rare phrases of Elizabethan English nor quaintly turned versions of Irish idioms. Its drawl was an echo of the quays of Dublin given back by a bleak decaying seaport, its energy an echo of the sacred eloquence of Dublin given back flatly by a Wicklow pulpit' (*P*, 199–200). Richness of language is repeatedly attributed to an interaction *between* languages. P. W. Joyce insisted that the vigour of Anglo-Irish derived from its duality, and *A Portrait* seems to endorse this position by neutralising Cranly's speech as an echo, that is, denying him any active role within his own discourse. This description reflects negatively on the language of Dublin, whereas Oliver St John Gogarty (the model for Buck Mulligan in *Ulysses*) found riches: 'There is nowhere a wittier, or cheerfuller, or more good-natured crowd than in Dublin. Profane, obscene, they come out of the Seventeenth Century with a power of expression that rivals, or rather, is that of the English of Elizabeth.' Gogarty attempted to realise this perception in his autobiography, *As I Was Going Down Sackville Street* (1937), which weaves together an extraordinary blend of dialect, obsolete forms and non-standard syntax. His enthusiasm smacks of the 'dear dirty Dublin' sentimentality which Joyce detested; on the other hand, Gogarty does make a point which increases the ambiguity of the title of *A Portrait*. 'Artist' in Dublin usage signified a 'quaint fellow or a great cod' and has been glossed within general Anglo-Irish as meaning a 'rogue'.[10] An awareness of Anglo-Irish usage, then, throws a very ironic light on Stephen's artistic ambitions, an irony which continues into his reappearance in *Ulysses* where he alternates between the would-be roles of scholar, writer and priest, realising none.

Stephen's relation to the English language is, of course, the most intricate linguistic issue of *A Portrait* and it can be helpfully approached via an argument mounted by Linda Dowling in her study *Language and Decadence in the Victorian Fin de Siècle*. She presents a convincing case that the style of late Victorian literature was decisively affected by the philological movement which had gained ground in Britain by the middle of the century. This science, Dowling argues, had a profound effect on how language was perceived: while philology 'made language visible, it simultaneously made language opaque, that is, taught students to see in language elements – roots, affixes, and so on – that referred to nothing outside the linguistic inquiry.'[11] Hand in hand with a new awareness of the historical dimension to words went a realisation that changes were taking place in a disturbingly autonomous fashion. Indeed, the main single impact of philological study seems to have been to induce a modern consciousness of the arbitrary nature of the word. In 1899 Arthur Symons introduced his *The Symbolist Movement in Literature* with just such a declaration: 'what are words themselves but symbols, almost as arbitrary as the letters which compose them, mere sounds of the voice to which we have agreed to give certain significations, as we have agreed to translate these sounds by these combinations of letters?'[12] Joyce was later to exploit this realisation to the full in *Finnegan's Wake*. In 1926 he sent Harriet Shaw Weaver a 'prosepiece', that is, an excerpt from his work in progress, together with a key which explained his method of multilingual puns. Drawing on both etymology and co-incidence, Joyce pieced together an enormously complex network of what Umberto Eco has termed 'lexemes', whose resemblance to English words becomes a springboard into other linguistic fields. Since no individual field is privileged, the very act of reading, of locating resemblances, constantly reminds the reader that the linguistic sign is arbitrary. In a far less complex way we shall see how such a philological consciousness also informs *A Portrait*.

The displacement of language from a God-given logos into the secular sphere left the way open for a materialistic theory of linguistic origins to gain currency. What was sometimes described as the 'orang-utang' theory that words originated in sensations was summarised by Richard Chevenix Trench, Bishop of Dublin, as deriving language 'from rude imperfect beginnings, the inarticulate cries by which he expressed his natural wants, the sounds by which he sought to imitate the impression of natural objects upon him'.[13] This view was popularised by Max Müller and was one which privileged word-roots in particular. Müller was a disciple of Darwin's and eagerly set about applying principles of natural selection to linguistic history from the 1860s onwards. In 'The oxen of the sun' episode of *Ulysses* Joyce was to apply the evolutionary principle by constructing an analogy between the growth of the English language and the conception of an individual. The occasion of the episode (an imminent birth) is synchronised with a pastiche sequence of prose passages from Anglo-Saxon up to the present day.

Just as the experiment in *Ulysses* demonstrates a familiarity with English etymology, so Joyce applies the sensation theory of origins to Stephen's stumbling attempts to attach meaning to words in Chapter 1 of *A Portrait*. Stephen passes repeatedly over the connections between words and physical sensation or objects. He lingers over the physicality of 'suck', 'kiss', 'click'; and begins to learn his first discriminations between near homophones ('canker'/'cancer'). Early in the chapter Stephen arranges objects qualitatively between two poles of cold and warmth, the former suggesting the strange and unpleasant, the latter all things familiar and comfortable. He constructs meaning by attributing voices to inanimate objects like cricket bats: 'they said: pick, pack, pock, puck: like drops of water in a fountain slowly falling in the brimming bowl' (*P*, 42–3). The sounds are articulated onomatopoeically and then translated back into the physical through an analogy which closely resembles Pound's 'Station in the metro'. Stephen is constantly trying to close the gap between words and things, but this can never happen. By retaining the third person throughout here Joyce reminds us that Stephen has come into a fully formed linguistic context. The monosyllables given here are therefore examples of what Bakhtin called the 'double-voicedness' of discourse, because we cannot read them in innocence of the conventions governing utterance and analogy. Nor can we blot out the consciousness that the words have meanings beyond onomatopoeia (which is anyway a codified part of every language). Joyce uses the four terms as a diminuendo introduction to the physical climax of Stephen's beating when the pandybat makes a noise 'like the loud crack of a broken stick'. In a very early form we are here witnessing a physical attention to words which will later become central to Stephen's poetical experiments.

Because Stephen starts lessons in foreign languages he quickly learns something about words which tugs in the opposite direction to a harmony between sound and sense. The following sequence is one of the most important passages in the whole novel:

> God was God's name just as his name was Stephen. *Dieu* was the French for God and that was God's name too; and when anyone prayed to God and said *Dieu* then God knew at once that it was a French person that was praying. But though there were different names for God in all the different languages in the world and God understood what all the people who prayed said in their different languages still God remained always the same God and God's real name was God. (*P*, 16)

God functions in *A Portrait* as a principle of order for Stephen. It is no accident that his remorse after the retreat leads to a systematisation of his life and thoughts. However, take away the transcendental referent (which is what happens when Stephen loses his faith) and words become floating signifiers loosely attached to meaning by convention or historical accident. In virtually every episode of *A Portrait* Joyce foregrounds certain words against their context for a variety of purposes, but always with the effect of highlighting them as words. So in Chapter 2 'tryst' reflects the impact of Stephen's reading in romantic fiction; and 'foetus' signals his growing awareness of sexual processes. In Chapter 3 highlighted terms begin to take on double punning significance so that 'retreat' also suggests Stephen's recoil from adulthood (he becomes a child over again), and he 'tells' his sins both as an utterance and as an act of spiritual accountancy.

In Chapter 1 of *A Portrait* Stephen's attempts to learn English are punctuated with gaps and absences. Understanding of one term frustratingly heightens his ignorance of others. So Stephen has a dim conception of 'politics', no idea of 'smugging' and is even denied the key word in Mr Casey's Christmas story. Simultaneously Stephen learns not only vocabulary but also the social suppressions that render certain words taboo. Chapter 2 traces out phases in Stephen's growing verbal awareness of the obscene as well as accent, dialect and scholastic theology.

Accordingly, the farther we read in *A Portrait* the more complex grows our awareness of the English language and a central principle of the novel's style emerges: words are repeated in such different contexts that their meaning becomes destabilised and rendered relative to the local context of their occurrence. So 'murmur' at the end of Chapter 2 suggests the heated inner voice of Stephen's sexuality. The succeeding chapter revises it to connote the outer voices of prayer and the inner voice of conscience. The more specific a word's meaning the more noticeable becomes its new context, and this is particularly true of religious terminology. Joyce shows in the central chapter of *A Portrait* that the Church possesses a cogent and systematic discourse, a kind of verbal articulation of its order. So when 'advent' occurs in Stephen's epiphany on the beach at the end of Chapter 4 the term has clearly been appropriated from its place within the Church calendar and transposed into the new sequence of Stephen's sexual/aesthetic awakening. Chapter 5 of *A Portrait* makes this transposition explicit when Stephen figures himself as 'transmuting the daily bread of experience into the radiant body of everliving life' (*P*, 225). Here the ultimate power of the priesthood and the stability of the term 'priest' have both been undermined by Stephen's choice of self-image. There are no fixed signifiers in this novel, where an 'event' can be a rhetorical displacement of this kind.

An important example of these semantic shifts occurs in the cries which punctuate each chapter. Sidney Feshbach has even argued that they form a rhythm in the novel as a whole:

> In each of *A Portrait*'s five chapters a cry occurs as the climax of a sequence of physical and psychological events that usually follow a single pattern or narrative rhythm: a situation ... provokes an internal response that intensifies until it forms a cry in Stephen's mind: the cry seeks expression and then, under increased pressure it is released.[14]

Feshbach is undoubtedly right that exclamations signal climactic points in the novel, each time with a different emphasis, and also that Stephen attempts to rationalise this in his theorising about the lyrical in Chapter 5. Each occurrence revises the meaning of 'cry' from a 'wail of despair' to a tearful plea for spiritual/emotional release and a spontaneous 'outburst of profane joy' in Chapters 2, 3 and 4 respectively. And always the verb signals the dramatic energy in the moment of verbalisation.

In the 1950s and 1960s much of Joyce criticism was devoted to examining what used to be called 'lines of imagery'. One of the classic studies in this area, William York Tindall's *The Literary Symbol* (1955) attempted to give a systematic account of a notoriously elusive concept and immediately ran into problems of definition. Firstly, a symbol was a 'visible sign of something invisible', then it was half of a metaphor and finally an analogy.[15] When Tindall's discussion really got under way the confusions multiplied as he slid from one term to another, from 'symbol' to 'image' and back again. One of Tindall's main texts for analysis was *A Portrait*, and he offered interesting comment on the recurrence of roses, birds and water in the novel, noting their variety of meanings. He sums up: 'These families of developing images' supplement the narrative and 'give it texture, immediacy, and more body.'[16] It is only possible to make this assertion because Tindall has privileged those terms which refer to physical objects. Like Hugh Kenner after him, Tindall declares that the opening section of the novel contains the germs of the ensuing narrative, but he chooses not to mention those words where the argument about immediacy or physicality would not apply. What term becomes more charged with connotation, after all, than 'father' from the sheer frequency of its recurrence? Each time it appears in the text it carries a slightly different emphasis whether on paternity, on the deity as originator or as a clerical term of address. As a foregrounded sign for a progenitor its implications multiply, so that in Chapter 5, for instance, Aquinas can be read as Stephen's intellectual parent. His biological father never quite drops out of the narrative but hovers in the background as a reminder of the continuing importance of his sign.

As these signs recur their mobility prevents them stabilising within a semantic system. This process relates closely to Stephen's loss of a naive faith in fixity in his childhood. When he later reflects on Swedenborg's belief in the 'correspondence of birds to things of the intellect' it is only because a fixed correlation between words and meaning has lapsed that Stephen can speculate about this relationship. He glimpses the sort of correspondence which Joyce wove into a massive network of systems in *Ulysses*, but because no one system of signification is privileged over the others the reader is obliged to manoeuvre between them. *A Portrait* uses words, therefore, as predictors or echoes and their meaning revolves to a large extent around a recognition of their repetition. It is likely that Joyce was influenced by George Moore's *Confessions of a Young Man* (published in book form from 1888 onwards), which uses the notion of 'echo-augury', that is, anticipating scenes and phrases. This method, according to Moore's editor, probably derives from Edward Dujardin's leitmotifs, which Joyce later acknowledged as playing an important part in the development of his own narrative techniques.

Etymology also feeds *A Portrait's* attention to the relative dimensions of words. In *Stephen Hero* the protagonist reads W. W. Skeat's *Etymological Dictionary* partly to build up the 'plenitude of an amassed vocabulary', a private arsenal of terms on which he can draw as necessary. In *A Portrait* this work is not named but is used substantially in certain sections. Stephen Whittaker, for instance, has shown that Joyce used Skeat to play on the etymological links between 'weary' and 'water' when Stephen is composing his villanelle.[18] At the same point Joyce is obviously playing on etymology when 'inspiration' is paralleled with 'inbreathed'. The cherished vocabulary of transcendental composition is deidealised by deconstructing the words into their etymological origins, stripping away the connotations which have accrued around them. The last chapter of *A Portrait* comments explicitly on neologisms ('platinoid'), survivals and anachronisms (Cranly's use of 'eke'). Words become a subject of discussion in their own right and this throws a retroactive light on earlier scenes and terms (Skeat notes that 'retreat' signifies 'withdrawal', for instance).

The episode which brings this concern to a head is Stephen's discussion of 'tundish' with the dean of studies. To Stephen discourse is always owned and the surface exchange on where the best English is spoken slides into Stephen's estrangement from English itself:

> The language in which we are speaking is his before it is mine. How different are the words *home*, *Christ*, *ale*, *master*, on his lips and on mine! I cannot speak or write these words without unrest of spirit. His language, so familiar and so foreign, will always be for me an acquired speech. I have not made or accepted its words. My voice holds them at bay. My soul frets in the shadow of his language. (*P*, 194)

Carol Shloss glosses this passage as follows:

> Stephen knows that English precludes Gaelic and that its ascendancy places him in history at a point where he, as a writer, can only borrow the words of one language and seek darkly for the older tongue whose use has been denied him.

> Caught between the foreign and the unknown, he locates authenticity in an unborn 'future' that his writing will help to create.[19]

This explanation comes too near to Stephen's sense of his own predicament to be really useful, for his detachment from language is sharpened by the not unpleasant implications for his chosen role as exile. In fact, denial of a 'natural' language could be read as liberating Stephen to appropriate terms as and where he wishes, whether from Elizabethan English, contemporary slang or Catholic scholasticism. In the diary section he looks up the term 'tundish', an action which suggests that the dictionary has supplanted the Bible as his textual authority. The passage above shows Stephen mentally striking a defensive posture towards the dean of studies' language, but it is only when Stephen recognises the alien nature of discourse that he can control it and therefore make it his.

Stephen's names represent a special example of how he relates to his culture and its supporting languages since they suggest religious and literary lines of derivation from Classical Greek. The first time that Stephen participates in a dialogue it is to answer the question 'what is your name?'. By foregrounding this issue Joyce makes Stephen's name a metonym of what Bakhtin has called the otherness of language. Just as language as a whole precedes the individual and supplies a context within which identity can be created, so a name is partly inherited and partly bestowed by parents. Within administrative contexts like Stephen's school a name is used as a convenient means of identifying an individual, whereas for that individual it is a given part of that verbal environment where her/his life starts. As soon as Stephen is questioned Joyce naturalises the strangeness of his name by making it a matter of internal discussion. Stephen's fellow pupil Athy temporarily disposes of the issue by telling him: 'My name is the name of a town. Your name is like Latin' (*P*, 25). Stephen gradually develops a sense of pride over his family name, which is mocked by his friends when they address him as 'the noble Dedalus', and much later in the novel there is a whole discussion of the pedigree of names which revolves around how Irish they are and therefore how far their bearers belong in Ireland.

Stephen's name also raises questions about how he relates to his context. When he visits Cork with his father he recites his name in an attempt at self-location precisely because he feels so out of place. Joyce further exploits the rhetorical possibilities of his name to raise questions about Stephen's future. Within the period when he was working on *A Portrait* Joyce began an article on Oscar Wilde by explaining that 'his name symbolizes him' (*CW*, 201). While Oscar was a mythical Irish hero (the son of Ossian) killed by treachery, the O'Flaherties were a wild tribe who constantly attacked the Irish towns. Joyce extrapolated from these Wilde's fate and his assaults on the 'body of practical conventions' as if in some mysterious way the names carried a prediction of his destiny. Many critics have noted that Stephen's family name derives from a figure in Ovid's *Metamorphoses* whose story is indicated by the novel's epigraph. Because this is one of the works Stephen studies, his relation to his classical prototype becomes internalised within the text, a matter for his own speculation, and he too wonders whether his 'strange name' carries a 'prophecy of the end he had been born to serve . . . a symbol of the artist forging anew in his workshop out of the sluggish matter of the earth a new soaring impalpable imperishable being' (*P*, 173). However hypothetical this possibility is, Stephen's thought comes ironically after he has been questioned on a quite different end, namely whether he has a vocation for the priesthood. Within the text these lines predict his resounding declaration of intent at the end of the novel. Beyond the limits of Joyce's narrative the intertextual ironies multiply. Stephen has been selective in identifying his classical analogy because he has selected only that detail which suits his artistic ambitions. In the *Metamorphoses* Daedalus constructs his wings to return home from exile in Crete, whereas Stephen is planning the opposite. Secondly, Joyce's epigraph ('he set his mind to sciences never explored before') continues in Ovid: 'and altered the laws of nature'. In other words, Daedalus is presented as an overreacher and the death of his son Icarus reminds him of the limits of his inventiveness and his helplessness before fate.

The last section of Chapter 4 makes explicit the multiple connotations of Stephen's surname. As he walks along the shore he hears the shouts of other boys swimming, but misses the analogy with Icarus ('Oh, Cripes, I'm drownded!') If the 'old father' to whom Stephen dedicates himself at the end of the novel is Daedalus among other significances, then Stephen is missing the most unwelcome irony in his name. The very title of Joyce's novel alerts us to predictive figures and the differences between youth and age; and representations of the Daedalus/Icarus story, like Rembrandt's for example, concentrate pointedly on the fate of the son, who drowns, according to Ovid, calling out his father's name. Stephen's imagination concentrates instead on flight (literally and metaphorically), whereas the myth raises its opposite as fate and bathos. Hence the alternation in the novel between rising and falling, between Stephen's exaltation at the end of Chapter 4 and the anticlimactic echoes of this scene in the sordid details of his home in the next chapter. Stephen's biblical prototype, the protomartyr, is also referred to at this point in the novel by the priest questioning him about ordination, and here again an analogy could carry fatal implications since Stephen's namesake was stoned to death for trying to spread the word. These connotations are brought out by the banter of the swimming boys, who play on the Greek etymology of Stephen's forename as 'stephanos' (i.e. wreath): 'Bous stephanoumenos'. Cattle would be wreathed if they were being led to sacrifice and so yet another hint of forthcoming death is missed by Stephen. To sum up we could say that his two names identify mutually antagonistic allegiances, to the Church or to his art, but in both cases Joyce extends their connotations far beyond what Stephen himself recognises.

Apart from its main echo of the mythic character, Stephen's surname is an epithet denoting artifice and skill deriving from Daedalus' construction of the Cretan labyrinth. 'Daedalus' was applied in Latin to artistic creation ('verborum daedala lingua') and in the form 'dedal' appears in Shelley (one of Stephen's favourite poets) to denote the intricate order of Nature. Similarly, Swedenborg, another theorist who Stephen reads, was referred to as the 'Northern Daedalus'. In *A Portrait* 'cunning' becomes one of Stephen's watchwords, which is simply an Anglo-Saxon substitute for his surname considered as a Greek epithet. Once we realise this semantic dimension then Stephen's experience becomes an actualisation of his name in a surprisingly literal way. The 'maze' of sordid streets with brothels externalises the complexity of his sense of sexuality, while later in the novel Stephen casts himself as a Franciscan heretic spinning out a 'lithe web of sophistry'. Now the maze has become intellectualised but in both these cases and throughout *A Portrait* Stephen's family name draws attention to the symbolism of labyrinths (whether internal or external) and thresholds. The recurrence of both raises ironic questions about the substance of his flight into exile which he prepares the ground for in his conversations with his fellow students in Chapter 5.

6

Stephen's University Dialogues

The prolonged discussions of aesthetics which take place in Chapter 5 of *A Portrait* capitalise on two notions of utterance identified in Chapters 2 and 3 respectively. The former places a strong thematic emphasis on speech as theatre, and the allusions to *Henry IV* noted earlier simply strengthen the analogy. Now idiolect and regional accent are foregrounded. Not only does Uncle Charles speak, but he uses idiosyncratic terms which are incorporated into the narrative discourse. Seizing on such details, Hugh Kenner has identified what he calls the 'Uncle Charles Principle' in Joyce's writings whereby his fictions 'tend not to have a detached narrator, though they seem to have because the narrative language becomes temporarily tinged with the style and idiom of the character occurring at that point'.[1] This stylistic 'contagion' is the consequence of other discourses' power to penetrate Stephen's consciousness, but in Chapter 2 he first becomes aware of style as such. The sections of this chapter each stress some aspect of performance: the first shows Stephen trying to apply adventures based on his reading about Napoleon and of *The Count of Monte Cristo*; the second contains references to pantomime and shows Stephen's estrangement from a children's party; in the third Stephen's father recounts a conversation about Stephen's 'adventure' at Clongowes, revising it into comic anecdote; in the fourth we see Stephen accompanying his father to Cork and here the Shakespearian allusions imply a similar detachment on Stephen's part from an embarrassing spectacle; finally, the chapter closes with Stephen's return to Dumas' novel, this time in relation to his growing sexual awareness.

The central section of this chapter concerns the Whitsun play at Belvedere. Stephen's allotted role is that of a 'farcical pedagogue', which, of course, anticipates his performances in Dublin. But if Stephen imitates the rector that mimicry is itself imitative of Stephen's own father, and an important theme in this section is Stephen's attempts to break away from any resemblance to Dedalus senior. The play itself culminates a more general and complex theatricalisation of Stephen's experience off-stage. He is given a mock-Shakespearian greeting by his friends ('here comes the noble Dedalus'); he notes the 'dandyish' style of a newcomer; and when questioned about a girl he retreats behind a façade of urbanity. His friend Heron accuses him of feigning piety ('you can't play the saint on me any more') and Stephen responds by reciting a mock-confession. The scenic correlative of this recitation is the transformation of Belvedere chapel into a theatre so that the performance of the play becomes a mock-Pentecost where the lines speak themselves. However, within the scene between Stephen and his companions is embedded the memory of a far tenser confrontation with other boys about literature. Here Stephen is the respondent not the questioner, forced out of his monkish role (his 'silent vows') by his commitment to the issue. There is a very striking difference in style between Stephen's words in the earlier scene and in that before the play. Where poise becomes all, Stephen had earlier fallen victim to his own enthusiasm for Byron. The narrative gloss at one point ('this thrust put the two lieutenants to silence') partially encodes the struggle as a duel between warriors, where the literal weapon (a cabbage stump) contrasts comically with its analogous sword. The literal scene drains off the heroic glamour of its Shakespearian echoes or resemblance to the arrest of Edmond Dantès, and it conflates religious and literary disobedience into a composite 'heresy'. Stephen falls a double victim since he lacks either the physical strength or the sustained verbal skills to defend himself. For the latter we have to wait until the last chapter of the novel.

Stephen's retreat at Belvedere supplies him with another model of utterance, namely exposition. In contrast with the scenes just discussed the situation of discourse is fixed and formal. The boys sit immobile and the clerics address them. As we saw earlier, the retreat consists of a series of such addresses; its impact resides in words not actions. And the clerics follow a systematic method of introduction, definition and amplification in line with the Aristotelian pattern of manuals of spiritual devotion. Even the sermon on Hell divides its subject up according to the different senses. In these sermons the shifts in tone of voice, the imagery, and the rhetorical use of questions whose answers are taken for granted, are all procedures in a formalised dialogue not addressed to Stephen individually (although he takes it that way) but rather to the boys *en masse*. The antiphonal sequence at the end of the retreat orchestrates through cue and repetition the acquiescence demanded of the boys, and concludes a sequence which shocks Stephen with a realisation of the power of the word.

Before we confront the specific dialogues in Chapter 5 we need to pause over the possible literary models Joyce could have had in mind when composing this section. The originator of the dialogue mode, Plato, follows a method whereby the dominant speaker (Socrates) takes his auditor from one hypothesis to another so as to induce agreement with his conclusion before the auditor has become aware of the argument's direction. The auditor is therefore present to endorse Socrates' logic, to call for explanation. In verbal terms the former's role is limited to utterances like 'true', 'exactly' and 'I cannot deny it'. Although this method obviously has a didactic purpose, it avoids monologic exposition by setting up a chain of propositions ('if A then

B') which are tested out inferentially on the listener. Joyce's two most famous compatriots, Wilde and Yeats, also made use of dialogues but in a rather different way.

Joyce's 1909 article on Oscar Wilde demonstrates a sympathetic interest in that writer as a victim of British puritanism, and there can be little doubt that he knew the dialogues collected in *Intentions* (1891). 'The decay of lying' and 'The critic as artist' use the dialogue form as a polemic against 'popular errors' of the time – the assumption that art must be useful, the privileging of art's moral purpose and so on. In each case Wilde uses a character (Vivian in the first, Gilbert in the second) to expound a modern doctrine of aesthetics using all the familiar Wildean devices of paradox (life imitates art) and epigram ('beauty reveals everything, because it expresses nothing'). The second presence in the dialogue acts essentially as a foil to this exposition and his role is to function as a one-man audience exclaiming at his friend's verbal and intellectual virtuosity, or to express cautious doubts about the other's ideas. He is more than a straw figure, since he partly represents the conventional attitudes which the main speaker is attacking, an external form of at least a notional other voice. In the duo Vivian and Gilbert it is the latter who particularly anticipates Stephen Dedalus in his capacity to produce throw-away quotations from Spinoza, Renan and a host of other writers. In 'The critic as artist' Gilbert explains the Aristotelian notion of catharsis to his wondering friend along with its subsequent interpretations by Goethe and Lessing, flavouring his 'lesson' with enough colloquialisms to retain the idiom of conversation. It is Gilbert too who comments explicitly on the dialogue form as being both ancient (deriving from Plato) and versatile:

> Dialogue . . . can never lose for the thinker its attraction as a mode of expression. By its means he can both reveal and conceal himself, and give form to every fancy, and reality to every mood. By its means he can exhibit the object from each point of view, and show it to us in the round, as a sculptor

shows us things, gaining in this manner all the richness and reality of effect that comes from those side issues that are suddenly suggested by the central idea in its progress, and really illumine the idea more completely.[2]

Gilbert traces the critical spirit back to the Greeks and here presents the dialogue as its best vehicle because it allows an author to play off one point of view against another. Because the author cannot be identified with any single voice (although this has not deterred many critics from glossing Stephen's words as if they were Joyce's own) it dramatises the play of the mind as an encounter between rival personae, and in that respect harmonises completely with Wilde's interests in the mask and in the theatre.

The final practitioner of the dialogue we must consider is W. B. Yeats. In *Stephen Hero* two works which lodge themselves in Stephen's imagination so strongly that he quotes from them are Yeats's stories 'The tables of the law' and 'The adoration of the Magi' (both collected in *Mythologies*): 'the atmosphere of these stories was heavy with incense and omens and the figures of the monk-errants, Ahern [*sic*] and Michael Robartes strode through it with great strides. Their speeches were like the enigmas of a disdainful Jesus; their morality was infrahuman or super-human' (*SH*, 183). To Stephen these figures become outlaws, heroes of spiritual revolt who feed his hatred of mediocrity; and in *A Portrait* Stephen again quotes Michael Robartes, although this time with less commitment. It is appropriate that Robartes should be cited in the chapter containing Stephen's intellectual expositions because Yeats used him and Aherne as personae in dialogues between different faculties of the self on different spiritual points of view. Josephine Miles has declared that the return of Robartes 'brought back not only the night but also the forms of conscious debate, as with Aherne, between lover and saint; it made the oppositions explicit.'[3]

Of the three stories which Yeats published together in 1897 'Rosa alchemica' uses Robartes to dramatise the narrator's division into selves, one registering pleasure from revery and the other observing sceptically. In 'The adoration of the Magi' Robartes functions as a prophet of the 'coming again of the gods', but the narrative enacts a disillusionment of the narrator's hopes, who by the end of the story is seeking to lose himself 'among the prayers and sorrows of the multitude'. All three stories enact a debate between desire and scepticism, between a yearning for the transcendental and an acceptance of worldly compromise. 'The tables of the law' more than any other could have offered Joyce an approximate model for Stephen's dialogues. It centres on two meetings between the narrator and Aherne who, like Stephen, has refused the priesthood. This gesture has established an independence from Church orthodoxy rather than secularism, and Aherne's role in much of the story is to expound the secret doctrines of Joachim of Flora, a Franciscan mystic (cf. Stephen's use of Aquinas and Jesuit theologians). These involve identifying a spiritual elite ('children of the Holy Spirit'), a sort of community of mystics who will withdraw from life. Since Aherne is stating doctrine the narrator's function is reactive (like Stephen's listeners), and when he expresses doubt or disagreement Aherne anticipates two of Stephen's favourite devices: namely, epigram ('Jonathan Swift made a soul for the gentlemen of this city by hating his neighbour as himself') and the citation of a different authority – in this case Leonardo da Vinci. When the narrator sees Aherne next on the Dublin quays after some ten years he has fallen into a depression from the frustration of his desire, and in that way confirms the narrator's sense of him being a type of the Irish race in turning towards 'desires so unbounded that no human vessel can contain them'.[4]

By now some of the main formal characteristics of these dialogues should have emerged. They locate themselves minimally in a grove or a room so as to limit physical movement as far as possible. A speaker in Wilde might light a cigarette; in Yeats he might make a movement with his arm. Wilde introduces both his dialogues as miniature plays with settings and dramatis personae. Physical appearance comes out in the Yeats dialogue because it contrasts two scenes separated by a ten-year interval, but in general the stress in all three writers falls squarely on speech. There is a common pattern of a dominant, instructive or challenging voice using the listener as a sounding-board for the ideas, a kind of preliminary individual forerunner of the larger audience which will be reached by the works themselves. Let us now see how Joyce incorporates this genre into *A Portrait.*

As Chapter 5 develops, dialogue takes priority over description, registration of thoughts and symbolism. Therefore this chapter brings to the fore the dialogical implications of earlier chapters. As different courses of action are discredited in Stephen's eyes the only avenue of rebellion left open for him is verbal. He must utter his non-compliance with the claims of Church and state, and so once again dialogue supplies a means of dramatising Stephen's relation to authority. It is not unusual for one particular character's voice to dominate sections of a novel, but we need to be on our guard against concluding that Stephen's utterances emerge from an inert context. Bakhtin has identified the aesthetic novel as a sub-genre where 'there is represented a speaking person who happens to be an ideologue for aestheticism, who exposes convictions that then are subjected in the novel to contest' (*DI*, 333). The particular example he cites is *The Picture of Dorian Gray*, where Lord Henry Wotton's epigrams (like 'to get back one's youth, one has merely to repeat one's follies') are examined by the narrative itself. Bakhtin's insight gives us a timely warning against overprivileging the authority of one speaker, and he shows how context can function dynamically. Lord Henry is content to view life as a spectacle, coining his epigrams from a safely ironic distance. Indeed, disengagement is the premise of his wit. Dorian Gray, however, tries to act out some of the former's ideas, with the result of fracturing his self into two disparate images. The novel, then, in a sense investigates the conditions from which epigrams emerge.

If we turn to Stephen we find that here too epigrams form a prominent part of this intellectual dandy's rhetorical arsenal. Who can forget lines like 'Ireland is the old sow that eats her farrow'? Jan B. Gordon has commented as follows on the epigrammatic component to *fin-de-siècle* wit: these aphorisms

> participate in philosophical reversals by doing the same thing to standard structure that parody does to its original genre: they enact their own truth in circular form so that the consequence is the revelation of content by form rather than the other way round. The oracular nature of the epigram gives it the character of *received* truth.[5]

The last of these points is most relevant to Joyce's novel since Stephen never manages the panache necessary for spinning paradoxes. He is far too guarded and parsimonious in his utterance ever to become a Lord Henry. On the other hand, he is clearly addicted to the authoritative style of definitions and definitions shade easily into epigrams. We need to examine next how this assertive or expository style bounces off Stephen's listeners.

There are six main passages of dialogue in Chapter 5 and each one reveals Stephen under a different aspect. In order of occurrence they are as follows:

1. A brief discussion of aesthetic matters with the dean of studies.
2. An exchange with McCann on signing a political petition.
3. An argument with Davin about Ireland.
4. A long dialogue with Lynch on aesthetic theory.
5. A group conversation on the steps of the national library.
6. A discussion with Cranly about Stephen's loss of faith.

The first of these passages functions as a preamble to Stephen's lengthy exposition of theory later in the chapter and also underlines one other striking difference between *Stephen Hero* and *A Portrait*. In the first work Stephen, like Joyce himself, presents a paper on art and life at the university which participates in a current public debate about the nature and politics of art. It is true that later in the novel Stephen makes a point of avoiding the college debating society, but nevertheless he has taken part in a public dispute. In *A Portrait* this possibility only receives the merest glance through the dean's suggestion that Stephen gets up something 'on the esthetic question'. Stephen's immediate reaction is to minimise (disingenuously) the significance of his thinking since his chosen arena is now private debate. We repeatedly witness him detaching individual companions from groups or withdrawing into solitude. Apart from that, the conversation with the dean implies that he is no fit opponent for Stephen since they constantly misunderstand each other. The dean merely opens up an avenue of speculation which Stephen pursues in his dialogue with Lynch.

Stephen's discussion of aesthetics has occasioned a lively variety of critical responses and it is fair to say that there is still no consensus about how to take them. Should his theorising, like that of Imlac in *Rasselas*, be abstracted from the text and then read back into it? James R. Baker argues that 'the emergence of Stephen's theory represents the climax of the young artist's intellectual struggles' and supplies a logical basis for rejecting Dublin as a place for creative endeavour.[6] Ellsworth Mason, however, is less impressed and sees Stephen's three aesthetic categories as the 'attempt of a very cocky young man to establish the extreme limits of his ambition'[7]. Failing to distinguish between the theorising in the Pola notebook and that in *A Portrait*, some critics like Haskell M. Block have even confused author with fictional character and read this section as straight autobiography.[8] One of the best discussions of this episode is given by S. L. Goldberg in his *The Classical Temper*, where he uses Stephen's statements to shed light on Stephen himself.

He declares that 'Stephen is intent on the dissociation of art and life, on the autonomy and integrity of the work of art in itself'[9]. While this can be justified as a reaction against pressure on art by Church and state, Goldberg also points out the drawbacks to this undertaking. In what follows I shall be pursuing a related line of tackling Stephen's theories as dramatic utterances in order to see how they fit into the general sequence of the novel.

First of all the obvious point must be repeated that Stephen's theorising transposes on to the field of aesthetics the expository methods of his Jesuit instructors. At the beginning of the discussion of Shakespeare in *Ulysses* Stephen reflects 'unsheathe your dagger definitions' and these definitions also figure prominently in *A Portrait* with all their tendency to hypostatise qualities. Just like the priest in the Hell sermons and *un*like the expositors in Wilde and Yeats, Stephen attempts an explanation by breaking down his subject into a number of components. The body–soul division in the sermons reappears as an opposition between higher and lower, between the refined and the dross. Even more importantly, we should notice the imbalance between Stephen's statements and those of Lynch in what is, after all, a dialogue. In Wilde and Yeats we encounter listeners who are there to express admiration for the main speaker. Lynch, on the other hand, performs as a ribald foil to Stephen's lofty attempts at instruction, reducing the latter's words to a game or competition. Although he is not a stupid listener (on the contrary, his comments are frequently shrewd), Lynch functions like an uncomprehending character since, as Bakhtin points out, 'stupidity . . . in the novel is always polemical: it interacts dialogically with an intelligence (a lofty pseudo intelligence) with which it polemicises and whose mask it tears away' (*DI*, 403).

Such an account, however, runs the risk of oversimplifying Lynch's role at this point. We have already noted how Stephen sees aesthetic apprehension as a process of detaching and refining. In the dialogue with Lynch he now attempts to formulate that process as a series of abstract propositions. He finds himself caught in the double bind of needing an auditor as an expository convenience, but actually addressing a figure who not only refuses that docility but who constantly raises obstacles to the flow of Stephen's explanations. Joseph A. Buttigieg has argued that Lynch 'fails to open Stephen's eyes to the tangible world of existential experience'[10]. In a sense, Lynch articulates a hostility in the very physicality of the environment to the 'course of Stephen's thought'. Joyce unobtrusively stresses the grey light, the smells of Dublin and the sounds – at one point a wagon of scrap iron drowns out Stephen's words. And Lynch's final words charge his companion with absurdity in trying to theorise about art in such a godforsaken island. Just as he reasserts a consciousness of place, so his responses constantly run counter to Stephen's main purpose, which is to evoke a 'mental world'. Where Stephen quotes Aquinas' theories, Lynch reminds us that he was a 'good round friar'. Where Stephen attempts to establish a refined or elevated tone of expression, Lynch performs a bathetic function by insisting on the body and on bodily processes. It is an early sign of what he calls his 'excrementitious imagination' that Lynch admits having eaten cowdung, and Stephen recoils so strongly from this thought that he momentarily denies Lynch's humanity, reducing him to a 'hooded reptile'. In fact, Lynch proves to possess an agile histrionic imagination when he feigns indifference to Stephen's theories at one point, shrewdly picks on inconsistencies at another or simply professes cynical materialism. He is a far more important and active participant in their dialogue than Stephen appears to recognise, and the latter therefore demonstrates a failing which Michael Oakeshott has pinpointed as a potential problem in dialogue. Every conversation, he explains,

> may suffer damage, or even for a time come to be suspended, by the bad manners of one or more of the participants. For each voice is prone to *superbia*, that is, an exclusive concern

with its own utterance, which may result in its identifying the conversation with itself and its speaking as if it were speaking only to itself.[11]

This is exactly what Stephen does. Because he grossly underestimates the actual necessary presence of his companion, necessary as a contrast and stimulus to his own expression, he falls into a state of self-absorption, where dialogue temporarily collapses into monologue: 'Stephen paused and, though his companion did not speak, felt that his words had called up around them a thought-enchanted silence' (*P*, 218).

This silence is deceptive since Stephen's arguments are designed to achieve the finality of truth. This goal, however, proves to be elusive since all the major dialogues of this chapter peter out inconclusively. To borrow Stephen's own terms, the stasis of final definition is eluded by the kinetics of a never-ending dialogue. We have already seen how much rhetorical prominence he attaches to definitions and epigrams. By their concise general nature they appear to stand out from their surrounding discourse. Stephen shows annoyance with Lynch at one point in the dialogue, when Lynch remembers the circumstances of one of his definitions at the expense of the definition itself. The very reverse is the sort of reception Stephen desires for his utterances. Accordingly, when critics detach his definitions from their context they are reading Stephen's statements as he himself would wish, not as the novel suggests. Just as Stephen quotes lines of poetry from his private 'treasure', so, like Wilde's Gilbert, he delights in citing passages from his cherished mentors. And during his exposition he composes what amount to intellectual purple passages ripe for quotation by others. This intellectual Wildeism carries a formal contradiction within the novel's context. While Stephen wants his auditors to apply, or at least quote, his ideas, for his *readers* to do so would be a violation of Stephen's basic tenet of static contemplation.

Unlike the three examples of dialogue discussed at the

beginning of this section Stephen's are peripatetic, and this fact immediately raises the possibility of an analogy with one of his mentors – Aristotle. The fact that Stephen expounds his theories as he strolls around Dublin implies that he is casting himself as that philosopher and also raises questions about his relation to the Irish metropolis. On his way to the university he reads the city as a landscape of literary associations and sees Trinity College 'set heavily in the city's ignorance like a dull stone set in a cumbrous ring' (*P*, 183). Because by the time he reaches University College Stephen's consciousness of place has receded critics have tended to put an overwhelming emphasis on his theories at the expense of how and where he expounds them. Place, however, should be taken into account, because Stephen's debate is ultimately with Irish culture.

Dublin can thus be seen as an extended stage for this debate. Take the university building itself. Stephen's entry is implied, not described. The emphasis is on a series of exits – from the lecture theatre, entrance hall and grounds. It is only as Stephen approaches the outside that he starts speaking at any length. Although a predominant image has been of him looking out through windows, now he looks inside from the street, sneering at the Dublin bourgeoisie in Maple's Hotel. Secondly, and much more importantly, Stephen's strolls around south-west Dublin convert the city into the grounds of an imagined Lyceum where Stephen plays the peripatetic teacher to his pupils. His model is Aristotle, whose *Metaphysics* and *Poetics* Joyce studied in Paris in 1903 and whose theories Stephen explicitly continues. There is even an approximate correspondence between Aristotle's esoteric dialogues and Stephen's with Lynch; and between the exoteric dialogues and Stephen's participation in the group on the steps of the National Library. Once again similarities are offset by differences, however. Stephen adopts an expository role at the same time as he recognises a national indifference to his endeavours; and his position under the colonnade of the library can be read metonymically in both intellectual and political terms. He stands neither within nor without his culture. So far as is known, there was no spatial opposition between the interior of Aristotle's Lyceum and the shady walks where the dialogues took place, whereas Stephen is traversing a terrain where all the landmarks carry historical implications. Does his pause on the library steps reflect a dilettantish rejection of the life of the intellect or a detachment from a national institution? The image ambiguously poises positive connotations against negative ones. Throughout the novel Stephen's phases of experience have been punctuated as an entry into 'some new world', whereas echoes of the past or ironic resemblances like the one just discussed collectively question the notion of novelty and show that Stephen's ambitions and spatial bearings are far more dependent on his past than he cares to admit.

When Lynch forces Stephen to place his definitions within a biographical sequence he is actually supporting the novel as a whole, which insistently places Stephen's theorising within a context. Whereas the latter is constantly attempting to emerge as an originator of novel ideas, the novel dramatises virtually every detail of his life, intellectual and otherwise, as a recurrence within a series of repetitions. The recurrent threshold metaphor which articulates Stephen's desire for flight in that respect carries its own irony since he is caught in the different phases of a protracted prelude which can only realised notionally beyond the end of the novel.

This generalisation even applies to Stephen's much-quoted explanation of the relation between the artist and artefact: 'the artist, like the God of the creation, remains within or behind or beyond or above his handiwork, invisible, refined out of existence, indifferent, paring his fingernails' (*P*, 219). As with virtually any passage we quote from *A Portrait*, echoes are set up here in three distinct areas: biography, religion and literature. The *deus artifex* topos (which Pierre Macherey has attacked for being tautologous: 'Man makes man') forms a local climax to one of Stephen's passages of theory and, being so foregrounded, Joyce makes it likely that the alert reader will pick up the relevant resemblances.[12] Stephen is giving an unacknowledged quotation from Flaubert's letter of 18 March 1857, where he explains his belief in impersonality. Stephen has lifted the central statement from the following excerpt: 'C'est un de mes principes, qu'il ne faut pas *s'écrire*. L'artiste doit être dans son œuvre comme Dieu dans la création, invisible et tout-puissant; qu'on le sente partout, mais qu'on le voie pas.'[13] Stephen's reformulation simply elaborates (or puzzles over?) the relation of the deity to his creation and adds an image deriving from Tusker Boyle, a boy at Clongowes. The concluding phrase to Stephen's definition stands out as incongruously concrete, and it is exactly this phrase which Lynch pounces on in his gibe that the artist is 'trying to refine them [i.e. his nails] out of existence'. The comedy of these sections grows out of a collision between the two speakers' idioms, and Lynch helps to reveal the presumption in Stephen's formulation by facetiously proposing Ireland itself as a creation which the deity has abandoned. The echo of Tusker Boyle carries implications of bathos just as the echo of devotional works elevates Stephen's assumptions to a new height of arrogance. For Stephen, of course, has a double ambition: to theorise about aesthetics and to become an artist himself. The desire to become in effect a deity contrasts ironically with what little we know of Stephen's actual output, and the allusion to a major nineteenth-century stylist only compounds that irony.

Context supplies signals as to how to read Stephen's pronouncements, and most of the indications in this chapter are parodic. The description of the physics class circles around the play between mocking and irreverent voices and the professor's scholarly monotone. The dog Latin the students speak to each other ignores morphology and semantics, and therefore subverts the scholasticism of the language itself. Interestingly, Stephen seems to have one foot in each camp. On the one hand, he will speak this dog Latin;

on the other, he will agonise over the niceties of meaning in Aquinas' vocabulary. Lynch and later Cranly mock Stephen's tendency to scholastic solemnity, but this style cannot be taken at face value. Maurice Beebe, for instance, has examined in detail the application of Aquinas, and concludes: 'Joyce follows the form of certain scholastic principles, but by denying the premises upon which they are based, distorts the meaning'[14]. It is not entirely clear whether this involves self-mystification or a subtle sense of subversion on Stephen's part; and, less ambiguously, F. C. McGrath has argued that Stephen's naming of Aquinas and Aristotle is a deliberate red herring to conceal the actual derivation of his ideas from the German idealists.[15] Far from being just another source-study, McGrath's argument attributes duplicity to Stephen's theorising and implies that he is engaging in an intellectual display where concern for truth takes second place to foxing his listeners. If this is so, and McGrath's case is a convincing one, then there is not so much opposition between Stephen's theorizing and the facetious counter-voices as there might appear. By attributing his ideas to the tutelary saints of scholasticism Stephen is subtly undermining that scholasticism, engaging in a deliberately heterodox act of revenge perhaps against the teacher who earlier accused him of heresy.

The debate on the origins of Stephen's theories seems a long way from refining itself out of existence, but in the meantime it continues to deflect attention from the nature and circumstances of their expression. In the dialogue with Lynch Stephen starts his exposition abruptly without any cue and violates a number of aspects of what H. P. Grice has called the Co-operative Principle.[16] Stephen speaks in excess of the information required by the situation, indeed seems oblivious to the situation apart from the fact that he has a single, none too willing listener. Grice's maxims of brevity and the avoidance of obscurity also go by the board as Stephen attempts to force Lynch into the role of pupil. Luckily for the humour of the scene, Lynch refuses to acquiesce to a purely laudatory role like the listeners in Wilde's dialogues. He actually interrupts Stephen to tell him he has a hangover and this initiates a whole series of interruptions which deflate Stephen's elevated tone and, by so doing, prevent him from producing an extended monologue. Stephen's ideal listener might be an even less oppositional figure than Socrates' auditors, but Lynch seizes every opportunity to be facetious, to bring the abstract down to the particular and to reduce Stephen's exposition to a fairground trick ('tell me now what is *claritas* and you win the cigar'). His refusal of turns and light-hearted interjections repeats the ribald comments of the physics lesson and prevents a decorum of utterance from gelling. Stephen's other listeners perform even more striking variations on this basic role.

McCann, a fellow student of Stephen's, figures prominently in *Stephen Hero* as a feminist and political idealist. He is based on Francis Skeffington, with whom Joyce published his pamphlet 'The day of the rabblement', and who produced a series of polemical articles in the *National Democrat* called 'Dialogues of the day'. Chapter XVII of the earlier novel (entirely cut from *A Portrait*) sets up an encounter in the form of a pseudo-Socratic dialogue, where Stephen uses the 'agile bullets' of awkward questioning to reveal the puritanism and inconsistency of McCann's position. The roles in this unlocated encounter are clear: McCann is the affirmer, Stephen the sceptic, only advancing a position of his own by implication. The reason for McCann's prominence is that he constitutes a potential rival to Stephen's intellect, and in the scene where he attempts to make Stephen sign a petition of support for the czar's peace initiative Joyce takes care to retain this dimension of confrontation.

However, if we compare this scene with its nearest equivalent in *A Portrait* a striking change has taken place. The latter is located in the entrance hall of the university, and is introduced by a preliminary discussion between

Stephen and Cranly. When McCann approaches the two he attempts to take control of the dialogue situation by encoding it as a meeting with himself as chairman. Stephen senses this and converts the attempted formality into comedy by making it explicit ('that question is out of order . . . . Next business'). As a circle of students gathers, a number of passing Shakespearian allusions (to *Hamlet*, *Love's Labour's Lost*, etc.) tacitly reinforce the theatrical dimension to the dialogue. It is fitting dramatically for Cranly to pick up a handball at this point since the action metaphorically comments on the dialogue as a game, and even raises yet another Shakespearian allusion: to 'bandying' words in *Henry V*. Stephen is obviously playing to an audience, but from the group of listeners there emerges a 'gypsy-like student' whose absurdly obsequious comments (calling Stephen 'Sir', for instance) deflate the aloof stance the other is trying to maintain. Joyce concentrates exclusively on the moves and counter-moves in this scene, rendering McCann's address on universal brotherhood in summary. Accordingly, the political occasion of the dialogues yields priority to the issue of whether Stephen can maintain superiority within that dialogue. This he obviously cannot manage, partly because of the gypsy student, partly because of the ribald disruptive comments from the other students, but mainly from his inability to withstand McCann's dogged insistance on signing the peace petition. Stephen tries to shift the debate from issue to style ('Do you think to impress me . . . when you flourish your wooden sword?': *P*, 202). McCann dismisses this point-blank as evasion, calls Stephen back to 'facts' and then mocks him as a minor poet. Here and earlier in the scene Stephen refuses to take up the cues that it is his turn to speak and lapses into silence. Neither McCann nor the scene in general allow Stephen to develop a sustained theatrical posture, and his only admirer remains the fawning gypsy student, an anticipation of Mr Best, who in *Ulysses* tells Stephen he ought to write up his theory of Shakespearian authorship: 'You ought to make it a dialogue, don't you know, like the Platonic dialogues Wilde wrote' (*U*, 175). Best naively misses a point which was surely not lost on Joyce: Wilde's dialogues incorporate within themselves an awareness of posture and stance which Stephen has not quite brought under control in *A Portrait*. Our acknowledgement of this weakness – yet another sign that Stephen is a *young* man – depends partly on our recognising the roles played by Stephen's listening friends.

We saw earlier how appearance was minimalised in the dialogue form, but, given the number of speakers involved here, Joyce has to distinguish between them and Irene Hendry Chayes has explained his method as follows:

> Gesture and clothing, details of physical appearance, peculiarities of speech, and intimate material appurtenances all serve to identify Stephen's friends in *A Portrait*, in dialogue passages which might be scenes from a play. Amid the profane, witty, or banal conversations of the students, the author intervenes only as a sort of property man, to mark each one with his objectified *quidditas*, which adheres to him from scene to scene virtually without change.[17]

To take only one example, the student Donovan is introduced through his physical size (his 'pallid bloated face') and his mannerism of putting a gloved hand on his chest before he is named. Through such devices Joyce creates a context for Stephen. The group scene on the steps of the National Library thus depicts the lively and profane (literally 'profane' since it takes place outside a temple of learning) banter of the students. Critics have scarcely bothered to comment on this scene, perhaps because Stephen recedes into the background, but it does in fact revolve around an issue central to his destiny – the questioning of religious belief. Here Temple takes over Stephen's prerogative as the witty mocker of religious solemnity and expounder of history. Now Stephen's apocalyptic intensities in Chapter 3 are reduced to their most mundane level. A fart is described as an angelic utterance; Revelation 6.xiii ('And the stars of heaven fell unto the earth, even as a fig tree casteth her untimely figs, when she is shaken of a mighty wind') is reduced to commonplace actuality in the figs Cranly chews and spits in the street; and Hell itself is dismissed as an 'invention' by Temple. Although the latter has an ostensible subject to speak on, his lines are constantly being interrupted with appreciative glosses by his companions. This scene presents a collective dialogue where students choose their own turns from within Temple's statements to play on names, extend his comments and act out a series of verbal and physical gestures which are relished precisely because they are theatre. Three times Temple tries to draw Stephen into the circle of their badinage; twice Cranly responds instead, and finally Stephen manages a rudimentary response ('is it?'), at which point the dialogue lapses and the narrative shifts into Stephen's consciousness.

The last dialogue of Chapter 5 is in some ways the most important, and is another denial of C. P. Curran's objection to the novel. When Joyce sent a copy to his former fellow student Curran complained that the students were not distinguished from each other: 'they all represent too much the same kind of foil to the only character you were really interested in'[18]. This criticism identifies a composite role and then lazily uses it to deny the obvious and sharp distinctions between, for instance, McCann, Davies, Lynch and Cranly. The dialogue with Cranly opens when Stephen begins to admit a quarrel with his mother about religion. It follows a question-and-answer pattern which, both speakers realise, resembles an act of confession; and in fact Cranly repeats the same quotation from Matthew ('Depart from me, ye cursed, into everlasting fire') as appears in the earlier sermon on Hell. Cranly carefully probes Stephen's words, again and again refusing his attempts to deflect questions into matters of vocabulary or abstract general truths. He relentlessly keeps the conversation on a personal level and exposes the contradictions within Stephen's attitude to the Church and his chosen fate as exile. Whereas Stephen's earlier dialogues are presented as a form of theatre, the speakers now are aware of shades of tone, meta-utterance ('Stephen . . . had been listening to the unspoken speech behind the words') and the connections between their words and a running revery (*P*, 246). The dialogue becomes positively Socratic at the points where Cranly tries to trap Stephen into admitting that following the observances of the church would cost him little, and yet the whole sequence movingly enacts the soon-to-be-dissolved friendship between Cranly and Stephen. If Stephen had not given permission and if Cranly did not know his friend well, the exchange could not take place. Hence the pathos of it ending on a discussion of the term 'alone' because it briefly raises the possibility that Stephen's very identity depends on an engagement between his discourse and that of the other students. Cranly tries to force Stephen to realise the implications of this word, and the dialogue breaks off just at the point where the subject has been actualised rhetorically, when Cranly does not answer a question. This is also the point where the novel shifts into a mode traditionally devoted to solitude – the diary.

7

Stephen's Diary

The change at the end of *A Portrait* to the diary form appears to offer the reader a unique confessional intimacy with the protagonist. Whether or not we agree with Hugh Kenner that Stephen has no one else to talk to in Ireland, the formal difference in narration is striking. As usual in this novel, however, nothing is quite what it seems. Michael Levensen has recently subjected this section to intensive scrutiny and points out the difficulty of it functioning as a conclusion because 'once begun, the diary silently imposes the obligation to continue.'[1] It is a genre, he tells us, which imposes not only intimacy but periodicity. Around 1904, at the suggestion of his brother Stanislaus, Joyce read Turgenev's *Diary of a Superfluous Man*, which is one of the most famous examples of the mode and which poignantly dramatises the difficulties of ending. Turgenev's narrator is an old man on the verge of death who passes away his last days recording his life-story. But the fiction of writing only to please himself gives him the licence to ignore narrative conventions, indeed to change his purpose from autobiography to self-examination and revery. It is only death which stops his diary and, as he foresees, renders it as superfluous as his earlier life.

There is a simple irony in the influence of this work on Joyce's novel because the latter describes youth with constant references to future ageing. The demise of Turgenev's protagonist is implied in Stephen's use of the diary form and implied also perhaps in Stephen's peculiarly intense reaction to an unnamed *old* man he records meeting in this section. The last two lines of the novel demonstrate how its periodic quality tugs against Stephen's own sense of the shape to his experience. The rhetorical invocation of 'old father, old artificer' (possibly deriving from the dedicatory poem to Yeats's *Responsibilities*) suggests that Stephen is poised between the closure of one phase in his life and the opening of the next, but the dating of the entry implies the continuation of a chronological sequence, an implication sharpened by the novel's dateline 1904–14. The many echoes of the past in the diary (of the bogwater at Clongowes, of Stephen's desire to 'forge' out an aesthetic philosophy, etc.) virtually smother Stephen's statements about the future since, as Levenson rightly points out, 'the novel . . . relies heavily on a formal principle that challenges finality with repetition and that encourages a view of Stephen as bound within a perpetually unfolding series.'[2] Far more is involved here than the convention of suggesting that life continues after the end of the novel. Levenson's shrewd argument enables us to see how there may be contradictions within Stephen's ringing declaration of purpose between future promise ('I go to encounter') and recurrence ('for the millionth time'), and between his ambitions as a writer and his tendency to quote from Shakespeare, the Bible and Yeats, among others. If his artistic potential is expressed through allusion and quotation the verb 'forge' takes on ironic implications quite different from original creation.

In fact, the diary section proves to continue the dialogic nature of the preceding narrative. It is one formal principle of *A Portrait* that the different sections bridge the gaps between them and this one is no exception. It begins after the passage of dialogue with Cranly which it distorts, as John Blades has shown; and it continues the notion of discussion through reported speech between Stephen and Lynch, his mother and other characters.[3] Sometimes quoting the speakers' actual words, Stephen not only gives us the debates (and they are virtually all verbal contests) at the time they happened, but adds another voice which continues them into the narrative present. So, while Cranly as a named character may recede out of the novel, the sceptical questioning voice he supplies is incorporated into Stephen's diary sequence, sometimes as a silent utterance in the interstices of the text. So the entry for 22 March begins: 'In company with Lynch followed a sizable hospital nurse. Lynch's idea' (*P*, 252). The last two words answer an implied question of initiative and, since Stephen in this section divides into narrator and protagonist, the phrase implies a capacity to see himself through the eyes of another. The elision of the subject pronoun is strategic because the discourse, as it were, moves between 'I' and 'he', between the self and the other necessary for that self's perception.[4] Rhetorically, the diary thus harks back to the opening section of the novel, where the pronoun 'he' can signify either Stephen's father or external versions of Stephen himself. Examples of this new-found awareness multiply throughout the diary excerpt. The discussions with Cranly, his mother, Davin and others begin as exchanges with named characters and then internalise the dialogue as debates within his own consciousness. This process is helped by Stephen's stylistic mannerism (an anticipation of Leopold Bloom's) of cutting off the subject pronoun from a statement, and by his use of responses which were not uttered at the time of the original conversations.

The shifts in pronouns in the diary section have a particularly important function in that they simplify utterances into the expressions of points of view. Locally, clear oppositions emerge between 'I' and 'he', between assertion and rejoinder. In the final epiphany of the novel the 'spell of arms and voices' is expressed as solicitations. First the arms speak through gesture ('we are your kinsman'). Throughout the diary Stephen attempts to negotiate a way through such claims without compromising his individuality, but the going can get rough, as in the following sentence (with emphasis added): 'Crossing Stephen's that is, *my* green, remembered that *his* countrymen and not *mine* had invented what Cranly the other night called *our* religion' (*P*, 253). Claiming possession, even facetiously, of part of Dublin runs counter to Stephen's general attempt at disengagement. Characteristically, place cannot be conceived apart from the Catholic religion and the pronoun 'he' at once refers specifically to Stephen's Italian teacher Ghezzi and to all those counter-voices trying to keep Stephen within the Church. That is why Stephen puts 'our' in implied quotation marks to distance himself from the collectivity. Within this general context of debate there is even an irony in the very allusion to Stephen's name since his biblical counterpart was known for his irresistible eloquence (Acts 6.x).

The diary form carries a permanent obsolescence within it since each entry lags behind the experiences which will produce the next one. The diary-keeper is thus, like the narrator of *Tristram Shandy*, engaged in a permanent race against time, and each entry stylises the author in yesterday's image. This is exactly what happens in Stephen's case since he observes his earlier behaviour with the sardonic eye of a one-man audience observing an actor. Throughout the diary he oscillates between histrionic projection, exclaiming in disgust over the shortcomings of Ireland and self-address, where ironic comment deflates the seriousness of the preceding lines. So whether the subject is his future career or his obsessive feelings for an unnamed girl who recurs in these pages ('O, give it up, old chap! Sleep it off!'), each statement becomes the occasion for a counter-statement; and so a continuous process of assertion and riposte is set up which stops rather than concludes. Not only do we expect an entry for 28 April, but very likely an undercutting of Stephen's solemn invocation.

In recording his own thoughts and actions Stephen becomes his own audience, implicitly observing his style for possible defects. When he is with the unnamed girl Stephen catches himself out in posture: 'Talked rapidly of myself and my plans. In the midst of it unluckily I made a sudden gesture of a revolutionary nature. I must have looked like a fellow throwing a handful of peas in the air. People began to look at us' (*P*, 256). Without necessarily identifying himself with the 'people', Stephen here comments on his own histrionic style and ridicules one characteristic ('revolutionary') by reducing it to a meaningless physical act. Stephen's commitment to his own stated positions now becomes essentially dramatic and looks forward to his elaboration of a theory of Shakespearian authorship in *Ulysses*. Now he has consciously adopted a costume of clerical black with his ash-plant as chief prop. Briefly arranging part of this scene as a playscript, Joyce colludes with Stephen's theatrical self-consciousness: 'Speech, speech. But act. Act speech. They mock to try you. Act. Be acted on' (*U*, 173). At the end of his exposition Stephen denies that he believes his own theory. In effect, he has been acting on his own mental cues to perform the role of an artist *manqué*.

The diary mode lends itself particularly to recording the process of self-examination, which it can only do by, as it were, dramatising the self as a separate character, an object from the analysing consciousness. When Turgenev's narrator asks 'what manner of man am I?' he continues: 'It may be observed that no one asks me that question – admitted.'[5] In the very act of denying one kind of dialogue he actually strengthens another: namely, an implied exchange between narrator and hypothetical reader, the latter being incorporated into the text as a silent but sceptical or questioning presence. In her examination of Turgenev's novel Lorna Martens locates a 'split between the head and the heart' of the protagonist which produces a heightened self-consciousness: 'He is preoccupied with himself and hence hyperconscious of other people's presumed assessment of him.' This leads in turn, as in *A Portrait*, to an assumption of direct address: 'His rhetoric is often that of one who is writing for an audience. He may be insignificant and mediocre, he seems to be saying, but he is also his own best critic.'[6] Stephen likewise sets up a dialogue between romantic assertion and realistic questioning, but certainly not from any consciousness of mediocrity.

Stanislaus Joyce himself kept a diary (strictly speaking, a combination of record, essay and self-portrait) during his brother's last years in Dublin and regularly allowed his brother to read it. Not only were James's reactions sometimes included in the diary but he asked to see it while working on *Stephen Hero*. The predominant purpose of this diary is analysis of the self. Stanislaus recorded the feeling of liberation he felt on leaving the Church because it enabled him to discover his own conscience, and he appears to have felt it a positive duty to try to understand himself. Accordingly, he diagnoses the same kind of theatricality as that which emerges in Stephen's diary: 'I am tempted seven times a day to play a part, and others encourage me by playing up to me. Let me guard against this and I may become something worth knowing.'[7] This record follows the learnt pattern of identifying temptation and bidding the self resist, but thereby produces a confession which is more honest than that which emerged through the sacrament. It is only through parodying the relevant sacramental procedure that Stanislaus can set up his rival text. Stephen adopts a slightly different tactic towards the same end. As soon as an entry is recorded he then questions it.

Stephen, like Stanislaus and Turgenev's narrator, becomes the reader and then reviser of his own text. Because diary entries are tied to specific dates, then, the main option for revision is diachronic, that is, in succeeding entries. As often as not Stephen disapproves of his style and so his discarding of passages comes to resemble a textual revision prior to composing some major work. At other points Stephen will not reject but rather elaborate the connotations of a word like 'free' – first used and confirmed in the entry for 21 March; or in the conflation of different 'wills' (suggesting both autonomy and sexual connotations) in the 24 March entry. Some of the entries are prose miniatures, occasionally based on epiphanies. On the night of 11 April, for example, Stephen composes a romantic nocturne which he turns against the following day: 'Read what I wrote last night. Vague words for a vague emotion. Would she like it? I think so. Then I should have to like it also' (*P*, 255). No sooner has Stephen dismissed his prose poem than he imagines a privileged second reader (with her name suppressed) and therefore has to revise his revision to bring his reaction into line with hers.

Although the inserted diary genre appears to promise intimacy, the above examples confirm Bakhtin's assertion that discourse is social. While the field of the discourse here is internalised, Stephen constantly quotes the words of others or lines from other works. These strategies demonstrate to himself (since he has now become the reader as well as narrator and protagonist of his own text) an ability to move easily from one intellectual position to another. So in continuing his debate with the Church Stephen draws an analogy between Cranly and John the Baptist, evoking the image of a severed head: 'Decollation they call it in the fold' (*P*, 252). This scholastic gloss places the key term within invisible quotation marks in order to distance Stephen from the community of belief which would use that word. The gloss also, of course, screens the self-aggrandising implications of the analogy. If Cranly is the precursor Stephen must be Christ, paradoxically a messiah to the very race he is fleeing.

The quotations and allusions secondly continue to feed a melancholy romantic self-image which Stephen simultaneously evokes and erodes. Once again dialogue comes into play here, this time between the formal cadencing of the more 'literary' passages and the clipped, sardonic or colloquial tones of their context. In effect, an interchange takes place between high and low rhetorical registers which looks forward to the parodic inflations of *Ulysses*. The style of the diary furthermore sometimes tugs against Stephen's stated intentions. The entry for 5 April contains the following: 'O life! Dark stream of swirling bogwater on which apple-trees have cast down their delicate flowers' (*P*, 255). The apostrophe signals a lyrical present, the 'now' of writing, and it is therefore almost paradoxical to place this figure within a narrative sequence punctuated by unusually explicit temporal marking. Furthermore, the apostrophe takes its place within a whole series of allusions to romantic endings characterised by languor, passivity and a yielding to death. Accordingly, they reflect ironically on his self-dramatisation as a rebel with a fixed programme of action.

The extended sentences, the appositions and the present tense of Stephen's purple passages attempt to draw out the connotations of words, whereas their context reasserts transience and transition in the continuing engagement between styles and voices. The diary section reads sometimes like a dialogue between the imaginative and intellectual sides of Stephen's psyche, between the dreaming and the waking self. In terms of discourse, this dialogue maximises the novel's earlier use of discontinuity and draws on the diary mode to authorise shifts from one style to another. If juxtaposition is the main device used for ironic effect in the last section of *A Portrait* then it is equally important to stress how Joyce draws on the novel as a whole for the materials of this section. Michael Levenson has pointed out that 'much like a satyr play, the diary recalls motifs that had been treated seriously and casts them in a comic light, tweaking the solemnity that precedes it.'[8] So exchanges feature Stephen's loss of faith, his interest in language or his relation to Ireland; and in every case the original intensity of the issue is reduced by a self-mocking remark or calculatedly prosaic detail which recasts Stephen's earlier positions as postures. What Ezra Pound identified as a counterpoint in the novel between inner and outer now emerges as an ironic interplay between perspectives. The retention of the third person throughout the novel has constantly reminded the reader of a perspective other than Stephen's. Now he depicts himself with a detachment which suggests that the novel was progressing towards this point of self-awareness. Stephen can now, as it were, appropriate the third-person rhetoric for his own use.

John Paul Riquelme sees the diary section as the culminating stage in the 'mutually self-engendering relationship of teller to character'. He sees the diary as part of the workshop out of which the novel itself will come, and therefore when Stephen is casting Cranly as his precursor the very nature of that act is to function as a precursor to Stephen himself. 'The constant displacement of Stephen through time', Riquelme continues, 'from the role of character to that of teller locates him as the primary element of the narration as well as the focus of the narrative.'[9] Through a self-involved argument which smacks of Stephen's presentation of literary fathering in *Ulysses*, Riquelme hypothesises an ultimate convergence of Stephen and narrator whereby the former will retrace the novel as the latter.

Where Riquelme envisages a circularity to the relation between Stephen and narrator, the argument of self-awareness could enable us to read the diary section as a culmination of the novel. However, Joyce's commitment to process militates against narrative closure. We have seen that the diary mode must continue and also that the principle of repetition operates right up to the last lines of the novel. The recognition of Stephen being poised on the threshold of a new phase in his life must be counterbalanced by the self-evident fact that he is reworking images and verbal details from his earlier life. The oxymoron of his 'new secondhand clothes' itself reworks a traditional trope for a writer's style to articulate this tensed combination of novelty and repetition. It has been a major burden in this study to show how, at every turn, Stephen's statements of self-liberation are articulated through details of the very environment he is going to flee.

The diary mode, we have seen, gives Stephen his first opportunity of narrative composition where he figures as both narrator and protagonist. The survival of four holograph sheets dated 1912–13 suggests that Joyce was considering an alternative ending to the novel. In these pages he introduces a vigorous mocking figure called Doherty, whose name is poised in between that of Joyce's original (Gogarty) and that of Buck Mulligan as he appears in *Ulysses*. Doherty's theatrical voice overwhelms Stephen's when he declares: 'Dedalus, we must retire to the tower you and I . . . we are the superartists. *Dedalus and Doherty have left Ireland for the Omphalos!*'[10] It would have been grossly inappropriate to introduce such a substantial figure in the novel's conclusion because the latter's whole emphasis is on taking leave of the familiar. Also it would have damaged the rhetorical unity of the diary which assimilates other characters' utterances as the counter-voices to Stephen's own assertions. *A Portrait* culminates at the point where the external perspectives of the third-person narration and Stephen's internal perspectives both meet in an area of consciousness which continues to be traversed by dialogue.

Critical interpretations of *A Portrait* which stress its progression through the styles of childhood to those of adolescence have performed a valuable function in demonstrating Joyce's patent adjustment of method to the different phases in Stephen's growth. It is equally important, however, to recognise that Stephen comes to consciousness in an already fully formed social and linguistic context. Any novel is, as Bakhtin puts it, an 'artistic *system* of languages' (*DI*, 416; his emphasis), and at every point in *A Portrait* we see Stephen manoeuvring through the discourses of his environment. These discourses exert such strong solicitations that they penetrate the most intimate areas of his consciousness and trigger not only a running preoccupation with language but a series of clashes between rival voices, whether they be the voices of the Church or of the flesh.

Characteristically, the novel progresses through these dialogical encounters, and *A Portrait* refuses rhetorical closure because, again as Bakhtin asserts, 'there is no first or last discourse, and dialogical context knows no limits.'[11] The apostrophe to life itself which Stephen makes in his penultimate diary entry in effect invokes all those addresses he will encounter by freeing himself from Ireland. The diary mode is strategically chosen by Joyce at this point in the novel because it too resists closure. The novel therefore ends on a note of prediction that Stephen's engagement in dialogue with others will continue. *Ulysses* picks up this continuity at a later stage in Stephen's life and ironically ignores his stay in Paris as a minor interruption to his life in Dublin. But that lies in the future of *A Portrait*.

Notes

PREFACE

1. Henry James, *Partial Portraits* (1888), Ann Arbor MI: University of Michigan Press, 1970, p. 381.
2. Henry James, *The Portrait of a Lady*, ed. by Robert D. Bamberg, Norton Critical Edition, New York: W. W. Norton, 1975, p. 175.
3. James Joyce, *Poems and Shorter Writings*, ed. by Richard Ellmann, A. Walton Litz and John Whittier-Fergusson, London: Faber, 1991, p. 211.
4. Oscar Wilde, 'Mr. Pater's *Imaginary Portraits*', in Derek Stanford (ed.), *Writing of the 'Nineties from Wilde to Beerbohm*, London: Dent, 1971, p. 212.
5. I have discussed this aspect of the novel further in 'Oscar Wilde's "Essay on decorative art": *The Picture of Dorian Gray*', *Swansea Review*, 3 (1987), pp. 42–55.
6. David Lodge, 'Double discourses: Joyce and Bakhtin,' *James Joyce Broadsheet*, 11 (1983), p. 1.

HISTORICAL AND CULTURAL CONTEXT

1. F. S. L. Lyons, *Culture and Anarchy in Ireland, 1890–1939*, Oxford: Clarendon Press, 1979, p. 51.
2. Arthur Clery, *Dublin Essays*, London and Dublin: Maunsel, 1919, p. 34.
3. George Moore, *Confessions of a Young Man*, ed. by Susan Dick, Montreal and London: McGill–Queen's University Press, 1972, pp. 57–8, 139.

4. Quoted in Lyons, *op. cit.*, p. 67.
5. Richard Ellmann (ed.), *Letters of James Joyce*, vol. 2, London: Faber & Faber, 1966, p. 187.
6. Daniel Manganiello, *Joyce's Politics*, London: Routledge & Kegan Paul, 1980, p. 39.
7. Malcolm Brown, *The Politics of Irish Literature*, London: Allen & Unwin, 1972, p. 386.
8. W. B. Yeats, *Autobiographies*, London: Macmillan, 1980, p. 316.
9. Ezra Pound, 'Affirmations VII: The non-existence of Ireland', *The New Age*, 17 (25 February 1915), p. 453.
10. Dorothy Van Ghent, *The English Novel: Form and function* (1953), New York: Harper & Row, 1961, pp. 263–76.
11. May Sinclair, 'The novels of Dorothy Richardson', *The Egoist*, 5, 4 (April 1918), p. 58.

CRITICAL RECEPTION OF THE TEXT

1. Breon Mitchell, '*A Portrait* and the *Bildungsroman* Tradition', in Thomas F. Staley and Bernard Benstock (eds), *Approaches to Joyce's 'Portrait'*, Pittsburgh PA: University of Pittsburgh Press, 1976, pp. 61–76.
2. Hugh Kenner, *Dublin's Joyce*, London: Chatto & Windus, 1955, pp. 117, 123 and Chapter 8 *passim*.
3. Hugh Kenner, 'The Cubist *Portrait*', in Staley and Benstock, *op. cit.*, p. 183.
4. Wayne C. Booth, *The Rhetoric of Fiction* (1961), Chicago IL: University of Chicago Press, 1968, pp. 329, 316.
5. S. L. Goldberg, *Joyce*, Writers and Critics 19, Edinburgh: Oliver & Boyd, 1962, p. 61.
6. Gérard Genette, *Narrative Discourse*, trans. by Jane E. Lewin, Oxford: Basil Blackwell, 1980, pp. 186–8.
7. Irene Hendry Chayes, 'Joyce's epiphanies', in Thomas E. Connolly (ed.), *Joyce's 'Portrait': Criticisms and critiques*, New York: Appleton–Century–Crofts, 1962, pp. 209–10.
8. Morris Beja, *Epiphany in the Modern Novel*, London: Peter Owen, 1971, p. 18.
9. Robert Scholes and Florence L. Walzl, 'Notes, documents and critical comment: The epiphanies of Joyce', *PMLA*, 82 (1967), pp. 152–4.
10. Richard M. Kain, 'Epiphanies of Dublin', in Staley and Benstock, *op. cit.*, p. 94.
11. James R. Baker, 'James Joyce: Esthetic freedom and dramatic

art', in William E. Morris and Clifford A. Nault, Jr (eds), *Portraits of an Artist: A casebook on James Joyce's 'A Portrait of the Artist as a Young Man'*, New York: Odyssey Press, 1962, p. 185.

12. *Casebook, op. cit.*, p. 194.
13. William T. Noon, *Joyce and Aquinas*, New Haven CT: Yale University Press, 1957, pp. 34–59; J. Mitchell Morse, 'Augustine's theodicy and Joyce's aesthetics', in *Joyce's 'Portrait'*, *op. cit.*, pp. 290–303; Haskell M. Block, 'The critical theory of James Joyce', *ibid.*; pp. 231–49; Shiv K. Kumar, 'Bergson and Stephen Dedalus' aesthetic theory', *Journal of Aesthetics and Art Criticism*, 16 (1957), pp. 124–7.
14. *Joyce's 'Portrait'*, p. 273.
15. S.L Goldberg, *The Classical Temper*, London: Chatto & Windus, 1961, p. 46.
16. Colin MacCabe, *James Joyce and the Revolution of the Word*, London: Macmillan, 1978, pp. 27, 64.
17. David Lodge, '*Middlemarch* and the idea of the classic realist text', in Arnold Kettle (ed.), *The Nineteenth-Century Novel: Critical essays and documents*, rev. edn, London: Heinemann Educational, 1981, pp. 218–36. This essay is also collected in Lodge's *After Bakhtin* (1990).
18. Maud Ellmann, 'Disremembering Dedalus: *A Portrait of the Artist as a Young Man*', in Robert Young (ed.), *Untying the Text: A post-structuralist reader*, London: Routledge & Kegan Paul, 1981, p. 201.
19. 'Polytropic man: Paternity, identity and naming in *The Odyssey* and *A Portrait of the Artist as a Young Man*', in Colin MacCabe (ed.), *James Joyce: New perspectives*, Hemel Hempstead: Harvester Wheatsheaf, 1982, p. 86.
20. Hélène Cixous, 'Joyce: The (r)use of writing', in Derek Attridge and Daniel Ferrer (eds), *Post-Structuralist Joyce: Essays from the French*, Cambridge: Cambridge University Press, 1984, p. 19.
21. Charles Rossman, 'The reader's role in *A Portrait of the Artist as a Young Man*', in Suheil Badi Bushrui and Bernard Benstock (eds), *James Joyce: An international perspective*, Gerrards Cross: Colin Smythe, 1982, pp. 22, 29.
22. Philip F. Herring, *Joyce's Uncertainty Principle*, Princeton NJ: Princeton University Press, 1987, p. 3.
23. Cheryl Herr, *Joyce's Anatomy of Culture*, Urbana IL: University of Illinois Press, 1986, p. 4.
24. Bonnie Kime Scott, *Joyce and Feminism*, Hemel Hempstead: Harvester Wheatsheaf, 1984, pp. 29, 135.
25. Scott, *James Joyce*, Hemel Hempstead: Harvester Wheatsheaf, 1987, p. 47.

THEORETICAL PERSPECTIVES

1. Richard Ellman (ed.), *Letters of James Joyce*, vol. 2, London: Faber & Faber, p. 99.
2. Tzvetan Todorov, *Mikhail Bakhtin: The dialogical principle*, trans. by Wlad Godzich, Manchester: University of Manchester Press, 1984, p. 110.
3. Virginia Woolf, 'Modern fiction', in *Collected Essays*, vol. 2, London: Hogarth Press, 1966, p. 107.
4. Julia Kristeva, 'Word, dialogue and novel', in Toril Moi (ed.), *The Kristeva Reader*, Oxford: Basil Blackwell, 1986, p. 37.
5. A. Walton Litz, *The Art of James Joyce: Method and design in 'Ulysses' and 'Finnegan's Wake'* (1964), London and New York: Oxford University Press, 1968, p. 12.
6. Roland Barthes, 'Theory of the text', in Robert Young (ed.), *Untying the Text: A post-structuralist reader*, London: Routledge & Kegan Paul, 1981, p. 39.
7. Kristeva, *op. cit.*, pp. 36–7.
8. Don H. Bialostosky, 'Booth's rhetoric, Bakhtin's dialogics and the future of novel criticism', *Novel*, 18, 3 (1985), p. 213.
9. Bakhtin, *Problems of Dostoevsky's Poetics*, ed. and trans. by Caryl Emerson, Manchester: Manchester University Press, 1984, pp. 233, 295.
10. Bakhtin, *Rabelais and his World*, trans. by Hélène Iswolsky, Bloomington IN: Indiana University Press, 1984, pp. 311–12.
11. Kristeva, *op. cit.*, p. 49.
12. The main comparisons have been drawn by Duncan Mallam ('Joyce and Rabelais', *University of Kansas City Review*, 23 (1956), pp. 99–110) and Claude Jacquet (*Joyce et Rabelais*, Paris: Didier, 1972).
13. Stanislaus Joyce, *My Brother's Keeper*, ed. by Richard Ellmann, London: Faber & Faber, 1958, p. 39.

1. STEPHEN DEDALUS' SCHOOLDAYS

1. V. N. Voloshinov, 'Literary stylistics II: The construction of the utterance', trans. by Noel Owen, in Ann Shukman (ed.), *Bakhtin School Papers*, Oxford: RPT, 1983, p. 119.
2. Michael Toolan, 'Analysing conversation in fiction: An example from Joyce's *Portrait*', in Ronald Carter and Paul

Simpson (eds), *Language, Discourse and Literature: An introductory reader in discourse stylistics*, London: Unwin Hyman, 1989, p. 87.
3. *Henry IV* Part 2, III.iii.36–7.
4. Thomas Hughes, *Tom Brown's School Days* (1857), London: Macmillan, 1920, p. 80.
5. J. Hillis Miller, *The Form of Victorian Fiction*, Notre Dame IN: University of Notre Dame Press, 1968, p. 64.

2. THE VOICES OF THE CHURCH

1. W. H. Longridge, *The Spiritual Exercises of St. Ignatius Loyola: Translated from the Spanish with a Commentary and a Translation of the Directorium in Exercitia*, London: Robert Scott, 1922, pp. 66–7.
2. J. H. Newman, *Discourses Addressed to Mixed Congregations*, London: Longman, Brown, Green & Longman, 1849, p. 380.
3. *Paradise Lost* Bk I.111–14.
4. Kevin Sullivan, *Joyce among the Jesuits*, New York: Columbia University Press, 1958, pp. 135–43.
5. Bruce Bradley, SJ, *James Joyce's Schooldays*, Dublin: Gill & Macmillan, 1982, p. 113.
6. Elizabeth F. Boyd, 'Joyce's hell-fire sermons', in William E. Morris and Clifford A. Nault, Jr (eds), *Portraits of an Artist: A casebook on James Joyce's 'A Portrait of the Artist as a Young Man'*, New York: Odyssey Press, 1962, pp. 253–63; Bradley, *op. cit.*, pp. 125–8.
7. David Hayman, 'The Joycean inset', *James Joyce Quarterly*, 23, 2 (Winter 1986), p. 143.
8. Quoted in Tzvetan Todorov, *Mikhail Bakhtin: The dialogical principle*, trans. by Wlad Godzich, Manchester: Manchester University Press, 1984, p. 73.
9. V. N. Voloshinov, 'Literary stylistics II: The construction of the utterance', trans. by Noel Owen, in Ann Shukman (ed.), *Bakhtin School Papers*, Oxford: RPT, 1983, p. 119.
10. Caryl Emerson, 'The outer word and inner speech: Bakhtin, Vygotsky, and the internalization of language', *Critical Inquiry*, 10 (1983), p. 255.
11. Cheryl Herr, *Joyce's Anatomy of Culture*, Urbana IL: University of Illinois Press, 1986, p. 234.
12. Bakhtin, *Problems of Dostoevsky's Poetics*, ed. and trans. by Caryl Emerson, Manchester: Manchester University Press, 1984, p. 195.

13. Sullivan, *op. cit.*, p. 145.
14. Dylan Thomas, *Portrait of the Artist as a Young Dog* (1940), London: J. M. Dent, 1974, p. 19.
15. C. G. Anderson, 'The sacrificial butter', in Morris and Nault, *op. cit.*, p. 271.

3. STEPHEN AS ARTIST: THE CONTEXT OF THE VILLANELLE

1. James Joyce, *Poems and Shorter Writings*, ed. by Richard Ellman, A. Walton Litz and John Whittier-Fergusson, London: Faber, 1991, p. 214.
2. Dylan Thomas, *Portrait of the Artist as a Young Dog* (1940), London: J. M. Dent, 1974, p. 42.
3. Hugh Kenner, *Ulysses* (London: Allen & Unwin, 1980), p. 8.
4. Bakhtin, *Problems in Dostoevsky's Poetics*, ed. and trans. by Caryl Emerson, Manchester: Manchester University Press, 1984, p. 198.
5. Michael Holquist, *Dialogism: Bakhtin and his world*, London and New York: Routledge, 1990, p. 60.
6. Linda Dowling, *Language and Decadence in the Victorian Fin de Siècle*, Princeton NJ: Princeton University Press, 1986, p. 206.
7. Arthur Symons, *The Symbolist Movement in Literature* (1899), New York: E. P. Dutton, 1955, pp. 71–2.
8. *ibid.*, p. 48.
9. Yeats, *Essays and Introductions* (1961), London: Macmillan, 1974, p. 159. On these parallels see George L. Geckle, 'Stephen Dedalus and W. B. Yeats: The making of the villanelle', *Modern Fiction Studies*, 15 (1969), pp. 87–96.
10. Symons, *op. cit.*, p. 2; Yeats, *Essays and Introductions*, p. 164.
11. Scholes, 'Stephen Dedalus, poet or esthete?', *PMLA*, 79 (1964), p. 487.
12. Yeats, *Essays and Introductions*, p. 157.
13. Jan B. Gordon, ' "Decadent spaces": Notes for a phenomenology of the *fin de siècle*', in Ian Fletcher (ed.), *Decadence and the 1890s*, Stratford-upon-Avon Studies 17, London: Edward Arnold, 1979, p. 36.
14. Robert Boyle, SJ, 'The woman hidden in James Joyce's *Chamber Music*', in Suzette Henke and Elaine Unkeless (eds), *Women in Joyce*, Hemel Hempstead: Harvester Wheatsheaf, 1982, pp. 3–30.

15. John Paul Riquelme, *Teller and Tale in Joyce's Fiction: Oscillating perspectives*, Baltimore MD: Johns Hopkins University Press, 1983, p. 75.
16. Symons, *op. cit.*, p. 39.
17. C. P. Curran, *James Joyce Remembered*, Oxford: Oxford University Press, 1968, p. 32.
18. Walter Pater, *Marius the Epicurean* (1885), London: Macmillan, 1909, vol. 1, pp. 94, 96.

4. STEPHEN'S DIALOGUE WITH THE FEMININE

1. Marina Warner, *Alone of All Her Sex: The myth and the cult of the Virgin Mary*, London: Weidenfeld & Nicolson, 1976, pp. 51, 336.
2. Sean Connolly, *Religion and Society in Nineteenth Century Ireland*, Dublin: Dundalgan Press, 1985, p. 55.
3. *Exiles*, London: Jonathan Cape, 1972, p. 175.
4. Suzette Henke, 'Stephen Dedalus and women: A portrait of the artist as a young misogynist', in Suzette Henke and Elaine Unkeless (eds), *Women in Joyce*, Hemel Hempstead: Harvester Wheatsheaf, 1982, p. 87.
5. Oscar Wilde, *Plays, Prose Writings, and Poems*, London: J. M. Dent, 1936, p. 226.
6. Henke, *op. cit.*, pp. 89, 101.
7. *Poems and Shorter Writings*, ed. by Richard Ellmann, A. Walton Litz and John Whittier-Fergusson, London: Faber, 1991, p. 184. In the 1904 'Portrait' the Virgin Mary functions simultaneously as a maternal presence and a spiritual catalyst, revealing the young artist to himself (*op. cit.*, pp. 216–17).

5. STEPHEN DEDALUS' LANGUAGES

1. Michael Bernard-Donals, ' "Discourse in life": Answerability in language and in the novel', *Studies in the Literary Imagination*, 33, 1 (Spring 1990), p. 56.
2. Umberto Eco, *The Middle Ages of James Joyce: The aesthetics of chaosmos*, trans. by Ellen Esrock, London: Hutchinson Radius, 1989, p. 18.
3. Dominic Daly, *The Young Douglas Hyde*, Totowa NJ: Rowman & Littlefield, 1974, p. 158.
4. John P. Frayne (ed.), *The Uncollected Prose of W. B. Yeats*, vol. 1, London: Macmillan, 1970, p. 255.

5. Stanislaus Joyce, *My Brother's Keeper*, p. 175.
6. P. W. Joyce, *English as we speak it in Ireland* (1910), Portmarnock: Wolfhound Press, 1979, p. 66.
7. *ibid.*, p. 251.
8. *ibid.*, p. 61
9. *ibid.*, p. 209.
10. Oliver St John Gogarty, *As I Was Going Down Sackville Street* (1937), New York: Harcourt Brace, 1974, pp. 25, 295.
11. Linda Dowling, *Language and Decadence in the Victorian Fin de Siècle*, Princeton NJ: Princeton University Press, 1986, p. 62.
12. Arthur Symons, *The Symbolist Movement in Literature* (1989), New York: E. P. Dutton, 1955, p. 1.
13. Richard Chevenix Trench, *On the Study of Words*, London: John W. Parker, 1855, p. 13.
14. Sidney Feshbach, 'A slow and dark birth: A study of the organization of *A Portrait of the Artist as a Young Man*', *James Joyce Quarterly*, 4 (Summer 1967), p. 289.
15. William York Tindall, *The Literary Symbol*, Bloomington IN: Indiana University Press, 1955, pp. 5, 12–13.
16. *ibid.*, p. 84.
17. George Moore, *Confessions of a Young Man*, ed. by Susan Dick, Montreal and London: McGill–Queen's University Press, 1972, p. 233.
18. Stephen Whittaker, 'Joyce and Skeat', *James Joyce Quarterly*, 24, 2 (Winter 1987), p. 189.
19. Carol Shloss, 'Molly's resistance to the union: Marriage and colonialism in Dublin, 1904', *Modern Fiction Studies*, 35, 3 (1989), p. 535.

6. STEPHEN'S UNIVERSITY DIALOGUES

1. Kenner, *Joyce's Voices*, Berkeley and Los Angeles CA: University of California Press, 1978, p. 16.
2. Wilde, 'The critic as artist', in *Plays, Prose Writings, and Poems*, pp. 49–50.
3. Josephine Miles, *Eras and Modes in English Poetry* (1964), Westport CT: Greenwood Press, 1976, p. 184.
4. Yeats, *Mythologies* (1959), London: Macmillan, 1977, pp. 294, 301, 309, 315.
5. Jan B. Gordon, ' "Decadent spaces": Notes for the phenomenology of the *fin de siècle*', in Ian Fletcher (ed.), *Decadence in the 1890s*, Stratford-upon-Avon Studies 17, London: Edward Arnold, 1979, p. 36.

6. James R. Baker, 'James Joyce: Esthetic freedom and dramatic art', in William E. Morris and Clifford A. Nault, Jr (eds), *Portrait of an Artist: A casebook on James Joyce's 'A Portrait of the Artist as a Young Man'*, New York: Odyssey Press, 1962, p. 185.

7. Ellsworth Mason, 'Joyce's categories', in Morris and Nault, *op. cit.*, p. 194.

8. Haskell M. Block, 'The critical theory of James Joyce', in *Joyce's 'Portrait'*, ed. by T. E. Connolly, New York: Appleton–Century–Crofts, 1962, p. 242.

9. Goldberg, *The Classical Temper*, London: Chatto & Windus, 1961, p. 46.

10. Joseph A. Buttigieg, *'A Portrait of the Artist' in Different Perspective*, Athens OH: Ohio University Press, 1987, p. 73.

11. Michael Oakeshott, 'The voice of poetry in the conversation of mankind', in *Rationalism in Politics and Other Essays*, London: Methuen, 1962, p. 201.

12. Pierre Macherey, *A Theory of Literary Production*, trans. by Geoffrey Wall, London: Routledge & Kegan Paul, 1978, p. 66.

13. Gustave Flaubert, *Correspondence*, vol. 4, Paris: Louis Conard, 1927, p. 164.

14. Maurice Beebe, 'Joyce and Aquinas: The theory of aesthetics', in Thomas E. Connolly (ed.), *Joyce's 'Portrait': Criticisms and critiques*, New York: Appleton–Century–Crofts, 1962, p. 273.

15. F. C. McGrath, 'Laughing in his sleeve: The source of Stephen's aesthetics', *James Joyce Quarterly*, 23, 3 (Spring 1986), p. 261.

16. Discussed in Ronald Carter and Paul Simpson (eds), *Language, Discourse and Literature: An introductory reader in discourse stylistics*, London: Unwin Hyman, 1989, pp. 150–6.

17. Irene Hendry Chayes, 'Joyce's epiphanies', in Connolly, *op. cit.*, p. 164.

18. C. P. Curran, *James Joyce Remembered*, Oxford: Oxford University Press, 1968, p. 63.

7. STEPHEN'S DIARY

1. Michael Levenson, 'Mode of writing and mode of living: Stephen's diary in Joyce's *Portrait*', *ELH*, 52 (1985), p. 1019.

2. *ibid.*, p. 1021.

3. John Blades, *James Joyce*: 'A Portrait of the Artist as a Young Man', Penguin Critical Guides, Harmondsworth: Penguin, 1991, pp. 126–7.

4. Michael Holquist, *Dialogism: Bakhtin and his world*, London and New York: Routledge, 1990, p. 18.

5. Ivan Turgenev, *The Diary of a Superfluous Man, etc.*, trans. by Constance Garnett, London: William Heinemann, 1917, p. 14.

6. Lorna Martens, *The Diary Novel*, Cambridge: Cambridge University Press, 1985, p. 106.

7. George H. Healey (ed.), *The Complete Dublin Diary of Stanislaus Joyce*, Ithaca NY: Cornell University Press, 1971, p. 33.

8. Levenson, *op. cit.*, p. 1028.

9. John Paul Riquelme, *Teller and Tale in Joyce's Fiction: Oscillating perspectives*, Baltimore MD: Johns Hopkins University Press, 1983, pp. 63, 68.

10. Richard Scholes and Richard M. Kain (eds), *The Workshop of Dedalus: James Joyce and the raw materials for 'A Portrait of the Artist as a Young Man'*, Evanston IL: North Western University Press, 1965, p. 108. The *omphalos* (i.e. 'navel') is an ironic double allusion to the oracle at Delphi and the island of Calypso, which were regarded as the navel/centre of the earth and of the sea respectively.

11. Tzvetan Todorov, *Mikhail Bakhtin: The dialogical principle*, trans. by Wlad Godzich, Manchester: Manchester University Press, 1984, p. 110.

Select Bibliography

WORKS BY JAMES JOYCE

Chamber Music	(1907)
Dubliners	(1914)
A Portrait of the Artist as a Young Man	(1917)
Ulysses	(1922)
Pomes Penyeach	(1927)
Finnegan's Wake	(1939)
Stephen Hero	(1944)
Exiles	(1951)
The Critical Writings of James Joyce	(1959)
Giacomo Joyce	(1968)
Poems and Shorter Writings	(1991)

CRITICAL AND OTHER WRITINGS ON JOYCE

Anderson, Chester G. (ed.), *A Portrait of the Artist as a Young Man: Text, Criticism, and Notes*, New York: Viking Press, 1968.
  Contains a number of standard essays, relevant excerpts from Joyce's other works and quite full explanatory notes.
Beach, Joseph Warren, *The Twentieth Century Novel: Studies in technique*, New York: Appleton–Century–Crofts, 1932.
Beja, Morris, *Epiphany in the Modern Novel*, London: Peter Owen, 1971.

The standard discussion of pivotal moments in Joyce's fiction and Modernist fiction in general.

Beja, Morris (ed.), *James Joyce: 'Dubliners' and 'A Portrait of the Artist as a Young Man'*, London: Macmillan, 1973.
Partly a collection of related letters, epiphanies, etc., partly a series of standard essays by Kenner, Beebe, Booth, etc.

Blades, John, *James Joyce: 'A Portrait of the Artist as a Young Man'*, Penguin Critical Guides, Harmondsworth: Penguin, 1991.
A sensible and thorough commentary especially on the novel's context, Stephen's character and aspects of style such as narratorial self-effacement.

Bloom, Harold (ed.), *James Joyce's 'A Portrait of the Artist as a Young Man': Modern critical interpretations*, New York: Chelsea House, 1988.
The latest in the critical anthologies, with some duplication of earlier collections.

Bradley, Bruce, SJ, *James Joyce's Schooldays*, Dublin: Crill and Macmillan, 1982.

Buttigieg, Joseph A., *'A Portrait of the Artist' in Different Perspective*, Athens OH: Ohio University Press, 1987.
An attempt to 'extricate *A Portrait* from the prison-house of the tradition within which it has been confined' by questioning critical preoccupations with pattern, stasis and the dogma of ironic disinterestedness.

Connolly, Thomas E. (ed.), *Joyce's 'Portrait': Criticisms and critiques*, New York: Appleton–Century–Crofts, 1962.
Contains a number of central essays on the novel and excerpts from book-length studies.

Denning, Robert H., *A Bibliography of James Joyce Studies*, Lawrence KS: University of Kansas Press, 1964.

Ellmann, Maud, 'Disremembering Dedalus: *A Portrait of the Artist as a Young Man*', in Robert Young (ed.), *Untying the Text: A post-structuralist reader*, London: Routledge & Kegan Paul, 1981, pp. 189–206.
A Lacanian reading which shows that Stephen's narrative revolves around a scar, a 'principle of structure'.

Ellmann, Richard, *James Joyce*, rev. edn, Oxford and New York: Oxford University Press, 1982.
The definitive biography, which is a mine of information about Joyce's works.

Epstein, Edmund L., *The Ordeal of Stephen Dedalus: The conflict of generations in James Joyce's 'A Portrait of the Artist as a Young Man'*, Carbondale IL: Southern Illinois University Press, 1971.

A detailed monograph on the tension between youth and age with valuable points about the father-figures in the novel.

Feshbach, Sidney, 'A slow and dark birth: A study of the organization of *A Portrait of the Artist as a Young Man*', *James Joyce Quarterly*, 4 (Summer 1967), pp. 289–300.
An elaboration of the theory of gestation as propounded in the Ellmann biography.

Friedman, Melvin, *Stream of Consciousness: A study in literary method*, New Haven CT: Yale University Press, 1955.

Gifford, Don, *Notes for Joyce: 'Dubliners' and 'A Portrait of the Artist as a Young Man'*, New York: E. P. Dutton, 1967.
Useful commentary, especially on the historical background and Joyce's textual sources.

Gilbert, Stuart, *James Joyce's 'Ulysses'*, London: Faber, 1930.

Goldman, Arnold, *The Joyce Paradox*, London: Routledge & Kegan Paul, 1966.

Gose, Elliott B., Jr, 'Destruction and creation in *A Portrait of the Artist as a Young Man*', *James Joyce Quarterly*, 22 (1985), pp. 259–70.
A discussion of the figure of chiasmus as it appears in the novel and the relation of duality to creation.

Greckle, George L., 'Stephen Dedalus and W. B. Yeats: The making of the villanelle', *Modern Fiction Studies*, 15 (1969), pp. 87–96.
Useful detailed account of Joyce's use of Yeats, especially of 'The symbolism of poetry'.

Harkness, Marguerite, *The Aesthetics of Dedalus and Bloom*, Lewisburg PA: Bucknell University Press, 1984.
The most useful sections of this study are those which document in detail Joyce's use of aesthetic tropes, images, and vocabulary in *A Portrait*.

Harkness, Marguerite, *'A Portrait of the Artist as a Young Man'*, New York: Twayne, 1990.
This work was unavailable for review at the time of writing.

Hayman, David, 'The Joycean inset', *James Joyce Quarterly*, 23 (Winter 1986), pp. 137–55.
A constructive examination of Joyce's 'insertion of alien matter' into the main narrative of *A Portrait*.

Henke, Suzette, *James Joyce and the Politics of Desire*, London: Routledge, 1990.
Incorporates her essay on *A Portrait* into a sustained analysis of gender issues in Joyce.

Henke, Suzette, and Elaine Unkeless (eds), *Women In Joyce*, Hemel Hempstead: Harvester Wheatsheaf, 1982.

A collection of essays on Joyce's artistic treatment of women. Contains an outstanding piece on *A Portrait* by Suzette Henke.

Hensel, Barbara Stevens, 'The problems of figure and ground in *A Portrait of the Artist as a Young Man*', *Centennial Review*, 26, 2 (1982), pp. 180–98.
Using analogies with the visual arts, argues that Joyce uses impressionistic and post-impressionistic techniques in rendering the phases of Stephen's consciousness.

Hodgart, Matthew, *James Joyce: A student's guide*, London: Routledge & Kegan Paul, 1978.

Joyce, James, *Letters*, vol. 1, ed. by Stuart Gilbert, London: Faber, 1957; vols 2–3, ed. by Richard Ellmann, London: Faber, 1966.

Joyce, James, *Selected Letters*, ed. by Richard Ellmann, London: Faber, 1975.
Both collections of letters are an indispensable source of information on Joyce's writings and are fully indexed and annotated.

Kenner, Hugh, *Dublin's Joyce*, London: Chatto & Windus, 1955.
Includes a pioneering interpretation of the structure and organisation of *A Portrait* which has survived the test of time.

Kershner, Robert B., *Joyce, Bakhtin, and Popular Literature*, Chapel Hill NC: University of North Carolina Press, 1989.
Makes an excellent start in applying dialogics to explain how Joyce's characters relate to their cultural context. Also contains intertextual analyses of Joyce's assimilation of other literary works.

Levenson, Michael, 'Mode of writing and mode of living: Stephen's diary in Joyce's *Portrait*', *ELH*, 52 (1985), pp. 1017–35.
Valuable narratological analysis of the diary section noting relevant sources and analogues.

Levin, Harry, *James Joyce: A critical introduction*, London: Faber, 1944.

Lodge, David, 'Double discourses: Joyce and Bakhtin', *James Joyce Broadsheet*, 11 (June, 1983), pp. 1–2.
A discussion concentrating mainly on *Ulysses*, most of which is included in his *After Bakhtin* (see below).

McGrath, F. C., 'Laughing in his sleeve: The sources of Stephen's aesthetics', *James Joyce Quarterly*, 23 (Spring 1986), pp. 259–75.
Sees Aquinas and Aristotle as red herrings and locates the origins of Stephen's theories in the German idealists.

Magalaner, Marvin, *Time of Apprenticeship: The fiction of young James Joyce*, London: Abelard–Schuman, 1959.

Manganiello, Dominic, *Joyce's Politics*, London: Routledge & Kegan Paul, 1980.

Morris, William E. and Clifford A. Nault, Jr (eds), *Portraits of an Artist: A casebook on James Joyce's 'A Portrait of the Artist as a Young Man'*, New York: Odyssey Press, 1962.
Another collection of standard essays and chapters from Joyce critics together with some relevant epiphanies and early pieces.

Parrinder, Patrick, *James Joyce*, Cambridge: Cambridge University Press, 1984.
Valuable general introduction which raises many issues, for example the relation of language to its cultural roots.

Peake, C. H., *James Joyce: The citizen and the artist*, Stanford CA: Stanford University Press, 1977.

Radford, F. L., 'Daedalus and the bird girl: Classical text and Celtic subtext in *A Portrait*', *James Joyce Quarterly*, 24 (Spring 1987), pp. 253–74.
On echoes of bardic tales in the novel.

Riquelme, John Paul, *Teller and Tale in Joyce's Fiction: Oscillating perspectives*, Baltimore MD: Johns Hopkins University Press, 1983.
A finely sustained rhetorical analysis which stresses 'the representation of the artist as character and as narrator, the linking of ends to beginnings, and the attempt to present the source of writing'.

Ronald, Margaret Loftus, 'Stephen Dedalus's vocation and the irony of religious ritual', *James Joyce Quarterly*, 2 (Winter 1965), pp. 99–101.
Brief but valuable analysis of how the priesthood figures in Stephen's choice of career.

Scholes, Robert, 'Stephen Dedalus, poet or esthete?', *PMLA*, 79 (1964), pp. 484–9.
A detailed analysis of the villanelle episode.

Scholes, Robert and Richard M. Kain (eds), *The Workshop of Daedalus: James Joyce and the raw materials for 'A Portrait of the Artist as a Young Man'*, Evanston IL: North Western University Press, 1965.
Reproduces with commentary a considerable amount of material subsequently incorporated into the novel.

Smith, John B., *Imagery and the Mind of Stephen Dedalus*, Lewisburg PA: Bucknell University Press, 1980.
A computer-assisted study which produces results of doubtful value, even as an explanation of themes.

Staley, Thomas F. and Bernard Benstock (eds), *Approaches to Joyce's 'Portrait': Ten essays*, Pittsburgh PA: University of Pittsburgh Press, 1976.
Avoids overlap with other collections and includes important essays by Kain, Anderson, Kenner, etc.

Van Ghent, Dorothy, *The English Novel: Form and function*, New York: Holt, Rinehart & Winston, 1953.

Whittaker, Stephen, 'Joyce and Skeat', *James Joyce Quarterly*, 24, 2 (Winter 1987), pp. 177–92.
Presents evidence for Joyce's application of Skeat's etymologies in the novel.

WRITINGS ON DIALOGICS

Bakhtin, Mikhail, *The Dialogic Imagination: Four Essays*, trans. by Michael Holquist and Caryl Emerson, Austin TX: University of Texas Press, 1981.
Contains the seminal essay, 'Discourse in the novel'.

Bakhtin, Mikhail (with P. N. Medvedev), *The Formal Method in Literary Scholarship: A critical introduction to sociological poetics*, trans. by Albert J. Wehrle, Cambridge, MA: Harvard University Press, 1985.
Contains Bakhtin's attack on Shklovsky and the Russian Formalists.

Bakhtin, Mikhail, *Problems of Dostoevsky's Poetics*, ed. and trans. by Caryl Emerson, Manchester: Manchester University Press, 1984.
An elaboration and application of the notion of dialogics.

Bakhtin, Mikhail, *Rabelais and his World*, trans. by Hélène Iswolsky, Bloomington IN: Indiana University Press, 1984.
Contains Bakhtin's famous discussion of the carnivalesque.

Bakhtin, Mikhail, *Speech Genres and Other Late Essays*, trans. by Vern W. McGee, ed. by Caryl Emerson and Michael Holquist, Austin TX: University of Texas Press, 1986.
Contains 'The problem of the text' and further develops the notion of dialogics.

Bialostoky, Don H., 'Booth's rhetoric, Bakhtin's dialogics and the future of novel criticism,' *Novel* 18, 3 (1985), pp. 209–16.
Brief but valuable discussion of Bakhtin within the context of an MLA panel on poetics.

Critical Inquiry, 10 (1983), pp. 225–319.
A critical forum on Bakhtin introduced appropriately by a dialogue. Responses appear in the next volume of the journal.

Diaz-Diocaretz, Myriam (ed.), *Critical Studies*, 1, 2 (1989) ('The Bakhtin circle today').
A very broad-ranging special issue containing contributions by American and European critics.

Select Bibliography

Hirschkop, Ken and David Shepherd (eds), *Bakhtin and Cultural Theory*, Manchester: Manchester University Press, 1989.
A collection of essays examining and applying Bakhtin's central ideas which includes a valuable essay by Nancy Glazener on feminist criticism of fiction.

Holquist, Michael, *Dialogism: Bakhtin and his world*, London and New York: Routledge, 1990.
One of the best introductions to Bakhtin, which situates his theories historically and which applies them to a number of works of fiction.

Kristeva, Julia, 'Word, dialogue and novel,' in Toril Moi (ed.), *The Kristeva Reader*, Oxford: Basil Blackwell, 1986, pp. 34–61.
A pioneering discussion of dialogics and intertextuality.

Lodge, David, *After Bakhtin: Essays on fiction and criticism*, London and New York: Routledge, 1990.
A collection of essays which focuses to varying degrees on Bakhtin and which includes a brief discussion of *Ulysses*.

Morson, Gary Saul (ed.), *Bakhtin: Essays and dialogues on his work*, Chicago IL: University of Chicago Press, 1986.
One of the best collections on Bakhtin. The pieces by Morson and Ken Hirschkop are particularly worth consulting.

Patterson, David, 'Mikhail Bakhtin and the dialogical dimensions of the novel', *Journal of Aesthetics and Art Criticism*, 44 (1985), pp. 131–9.
An article which argues 'that the dialogical dimensions of the novel are the spiritual dimensions of the novel and of life itself'.

Shukman, Ann (ed.), *Bakhtin School Papers*, Somerton, Oxford: RPT, 1983.
An important collection of essays by Medvedev and Bakhtin, those by the latter written under other names.

Studies in the Literary Imagination, 33, 1 (Spring 1990).
A special Bakhtin issue which contains valuable discussions of dialogism in relation to poetry (David H. Richter) and heteroglossia as a means of explaining the transactions of public life (Ken Hirschkop). Lennard J. Davis has trenchant charges to level against some of Bakhtin's central theories.

Todorov, Tzvetan, *Mikhail Bakhtin: The dialogical principle*, trans. by Wlad Godzich, Manchester: Manchester University Press, 1984.
Invaluable commentary on the dimensions of utterance, Bakhtin's notion of genre, etc.

Index

Index

Index

Oakeshott, Michael, 153–4, 183n
Ovid, 123, 140–1

Parnell, C.S., 10–11, 51, 105–6, 128
Pater, Walter, x, 75, 80, 98, 101–2
philological movement, 131–3, 138, 182n
Pinamonti, Giovanni, 66
Plato, 145–6, 159, 163
Pound, Ezra, 9, 12, 16, 133, 171, 176n

Rabelais, François, 39, 178n
Richardson, Dorothy, 14, 176n
Rimband, Jean-Arthur, 99

Shakespeare, William, 51, 63–4, 104, 143–4, 152, 160, 165, 168, 179n
Shaw, G.B., 7
Shelley, P.B., 9, 52, 89, 142
Sinclair, May, 14, 176n
Skeat, W.W., 138, 182n
Socrates, 145–6, 159, 163
Stevenson, R.L., ix
stream of consciousness, 13–14, 17–18, 30
Swedenborg, Emmanuel, 99, 101, 137, 142
Swift, Jonathan, 148

Symbolist movement, 87–90, 96, 98–9, 132, 180n, 182n
Symons, Arthur, 81, 87–90, 99, 132, 180n, 182n
Synge, John, 5

Thomas, Dylan, 77–8, 83, 180n
Tinayre, Marcelle, 106
Todorov, Tzvetan, 29, 32, 178n, 184n
Tolstoy, Leo, 37–8
Trench, R.C., 132–3, 182n
Turgenev, Ivan, 164–5, 169, 184n

Virgin Mary, 61–2, 65, 74, 90, 93, 95, 103–6, 109–13, 118–20, 181n
Voloshinov, V.N., 48, 71, 178n, 179n

Warner, Marina, 103–4, 181n
Wilde, Oscar, x, 11, 107–8, 111, 140, 146–50, 152, 154, 161, 175n, 181n
Woolf, Virginia, 20, 30, 178n

Yeats, W.B., 4–6, 8–11, 80, 81, 85, 88–90, 92–3, 98, 100, 101, 124–5, 146–9, 152, 165, 176n, 180n, 181n, 182n